DUKE ELLINGTON

DUKE ELLINGTON
James Lincoln Collier

COLLIER BOOKS

Macmillan Publishing Company   *New York*
Maxwell Macmillan Canada   *Toronto*
Maxwell Macmillan International
New York   Oxford   Singapore   Sydney

Collier Books
Macmillan Publishing Company
866 Third Avenue
New York, NY 10022

Maxwell Macmillan Canada, Inc.
1200 Eglinton Avenue East
Suite 200
Don Mills, Ontario M3C 3N1

Macmillan Publishing Company is part of the Maxwell Communication
Group of Companies.
Printed in the United States of America
10 9 8 7 6 5 4 3 2 1
The text of this book is set in 11 pt. Fairfield Medium.
A hardcover edition of Duke Ellington is available from
Macmillan Publishing Company.

Library of Congress Cataloging-in-Publication Data
Collier, James Lincoln, date.
Duke Ellington / James Lincoln Collier.—1st Collier Books ed.
p. cm.
Originally published: New York: Macmillan, © 1991.
Includes bibliographical references and index.
Summary: Traces the life of the internationally acclaimed musician and
composer who helped popularize jazz music.
ISBN 0-02-042675-5
1. Ellington, Duke, 1899–1974—Juvenile literature.
2. Musicians—United States—Biography—Juvenile literature.
3. Afro-American musicians—Biography—Juvenile literature.
[1. Ellington, Duke, 1899–1974. 2. Musicians. 3. Composers.
4. Afro-Americans—Biography.] I. Title.
ML3930.E44C6 1993
781.65'092—dc20
[B]   92-39793

FOR JANET

CONTENTS

CHAPTER ONE

He is a boy of about twelve, coming down the stairs of his home in the morning, ready to leave for school. Halfway down he pauses and looks over the banister to his mother and father below. "It is the great and glorious Duke Ellington," he announces in grandiloquent tones. He makes a deep bow and straightens up. "Applaud," he demands. Obediently his parents clap their hands. Then he skitters down the stairs and runs off to school.

It is a scene that was played out many times by the young Duke Ellington. Often he told his mother, "Your son is going to be the greatest, the grandest, the most glorious Duke." Sometimes when his younger female cousins were visiting, he would stand on the stoop in front of the house and order them to curtsey to him. Years later one of them remembered how angry she would get when Duke would command her to stand at attention, and then curtsy while he walked down the front steps. But she did it anyway, for Duke, even as a boy, had a presence that people were forced to respect. Already as a youngster, Duke was practicing at being famous.

But famous at what? He did not know, nor did anyone suspect what it might be. He would be famous, that was all.

Most people who go on to become great musicians are called to it early. Louis Armstrong, who had as profound an impact on American music as Ellington would, was determined to become a musician before he owned a musical instrument of his own, and the great German composer Wolfgang Amadeus Mozart was composing when he was six years old. Geniuses like these seem to have been born with a special talent.

But Duke Ellington was different. He was not a "born genius," like Louis Armstrong; he was instead a "made" genius—sculpted over time by chance, circumstances, and the sort of person he was. That is to say, being a certain kind of person, Duke reacted to what was going on around him in a certain way; and it led him almost inevitably step-by-step to become perhaps the most important figure in American music of the twentieth century. In this book we will try to see how this came about, how Duke took those steps which on his death caused the *New York Times* to call him "America's greatest composer."

We must begin with the fact that Duke was black, growing up at a time when being black was a far more difficult matter than it is today. At that time blacks were almost universally "segregated" from the mainstream of American life. This segregation was official in the South, where blacks were not allowed to use bathrooms reserved for whites; could not eat in ordinary restaurants, but must go to their own black ones; had to occupy special seats away from whites on buses and trains; and faced other kinds of indignities as a part of their daily lives. In the North segregation was not official, but it existed none-

10

theless. Blacks were expected to live in their own neighborhoods where they would have their own schools, shops, banks, and the rest. It was rare even in big northern cities, with large black populations, to see blacks in shops, restaurants, or bars outside of the black areas.

Moreover, everything in black neighborhoods was in worse condition, more run-down, generally poorer from what was acceptable in white neighborhoods. Black schools were given less money to operate on than white schools. The buildings, playground and other equipment were almost always in bad condition. Their textbooks were frequently ones that had been worn out by white students. Furthermore, white colleges and universities were reluctant to accept very many blacks. Some northern colleges took in a few token blacks, and a very few places, like Oberlin College, had a tradition of admitting a good many black students. But as a rule it was difficult for a black to get a good education.

And even those blacks who did manage to educate themselves found their ways barred to most businesses and professions. It was virtually impossible for a black to get a job in a white bank, a white law firm, or a white architect's office, except as a mopper of floors or a washer of windows.

As astonishing as it may seem today, at the time Ellington was growing up blacks were also banned from white athletic teams. A very few blacks, like the famous Jack Johnson, became boxing champions; a few blacks, in the early days, played professional football; and a few others, like Jesse Owens who was the hero of the 1936 Olympic Games, made their ways into other sports. But as a rule blacks were confined to their own teams and leagues until 1947, when Jackie Robinson became a star for the Brooklyn Dodgers baseball team.

So it went everywhere. In business, the professions, education, government, politics, and everything else, blacks were accepted only in small numbers on sufferance, or actually banned by law or custom.

The consequence was that blacks had to form their own separate institutions to run alongside the white ones. Thus, in the years after the Civil War, there grew up black colleges and universities, like Howard University in Washington, D.C., and the famous Tuskegee Institute in Tuskegee, Alabama. Blacks started their own businesses, like banks, insurance companies, funeral parlors, barbershops, legal and medical offices. They organized their own athletic leagues, with teams like the well-known Negro Giants, who could give the best white teams a good battle. They started their own labor unions, such as the Brotherhood of Railroad Porters, which eventually gave its well-known chief, A. Philip Randolph, some political influence with the national government. Everywhere in American life there existed these black institutions which ran parallel to the white ones. But they were always secondary to the white ones. Black universities, baseball teams, and unions did not have the numbers of people, the money, nor the influence to match the white ones. Blacks, therefore, were not getting a fair slice of the American pie; it was always just a sliver.

Washington, D.C., where Duke Ellington grew up, was a little different. Howard University, with its black professors and scholars was there. There were also blacks working for the United States government, a few of them in fairly important jobs. There was a large group of black professionals in Washington, including many black doctors and lawyers. As a consequence of all of this, there existed in Washington an upper crust of well-educated, professional blacks, who set the tone for the black community as a whole. To be sure, there were thousands of other blacks living in the worst kind of poverty in back alley shanties; but as a boy, Duke did not see much of this underside of black life. He would grow up in the midst of a large and quite proud community of middle-class blacks, which was seen by many blacks elsewhere as being special.

The key word here is *proud*. Years later Duke would explain that in school he and his fellow students were taught "that proper speech and good manners were our first obligations, because as representatives of the Negro race we were to command respect for our people." He was taught black history along with his regular courses. His school instilled in the students a sense of racial pride, not merely that they were as good as anybody else, but that they were better than a good many people. Ellington insisted that at one point the city of Washington wanted to integrate his school, and it was the black parents who resisted, because they were afraid the white kids who would come into the school might not be good enough to mix with their children. This pride in himself as a man, a black, and a human being was something instilled in Duke from the beginning as a result of growing up in the solid black community that then existed in Washington. This attitude would have profound effects on what was to become of him.

Even more important to him than the society that shaped him was the family he grew up in. His mother, Daisy Kennedy, had been born and raised in the upper levels of Washington's black society. Her father, James William Kennedy, was a captain of police in the city, an important job for a black to have obtained at the time. He had a great deal of prestige and not a little power in the black community. Moreover, Daisy was a beautiful young woman. She was properly raised to be respectable—to carry herself with dignity, to dress properly, to be able to carry on a polite conversation with anybody. We must remember that the spirit of those times was different: Young women from respectable families would not think of swearing, talking about sex, drinking, or smoking. This was the way Daisy Kennedy was brought up. She studied the piano, because young women were supposed to have an artistic side, and she mingled with the sons and daughters of the black professionals of the city. She might well have married a young professor from Howard University, or one of the sons of the doctors and lawyers in her social group. But she chose a different kind of man.

Duke Ellington's father, James Edward Ellington, who was usually called J.E., was born to a large family living on a small farm in North Carolina. He did not get much education, but he did get some, and in time he developed a rather elegant manner of speech, dress, and deportment which would rub off on his son. However, times were bad in the South when he was young. Agriculture was depressed, and making matters worse, many southern states were pushing through "Jim Crow" laws, drawing the noose of segregation ever tighter around black necks. Many blacks chose to move north, and J.E. was one of them.

Washington was a logical destination from North Carolina. He arrived in that city when he was still in his teens, and began working in menial jobs, probably as a dishwasher or cleaner in restaurants. He was, however, intelligent, ambitious, and well-mannered. He soon got a job as coachman to a prominent white doctor, and in time worked his way up to become butler for the family. This job probably required him to oversee some of the other servants, and to see that things ran smoothly in the household. J.E. quickly became knowledgeable about the best wines, fine chinaware, and how to serve an elegant dinner party. He knew how a gentleman dressed, how he lived, how he carried himself, and he was determined to live like a gentleman himself if he could manage it. A good deal of what Duke Ellington would become grew out of J.E.'s determination to be somebody.

Even though Daisy Kennedy could have married somebody

higher up the social scale than J.E., she must have been attracted by his wit and his manner. They married, and on April 29, 1899, Daisy gave birth to a son whom they named Edward Kennedy Ellington.

J.E. and Daisy were by no means wealthy. Daisy sometimes helped out at parties given by J.E.'s employer in order to bring in extra money. But compared to most American blacks, and many white Americans as well, the family was comfortably off. There was always plenty of food and drink, and if Duke's clothes were occasionally patched, they were always clean and well pressed. Daisy never had to work full-time—in those days most mothers, except the poorest, did not work, but stayed home with the children. In the summers J.E. would send his family to the seashore to escape the big city heat. Perhaps most important, Daisy had many relatives in Washington, and so did J.E., for several of his brothers had also migrated to Washington from North Carolina. On Sundays Duke and his cousin Sonny used to make the rounds of the families, being especially careful to visit houses where his aunts and uncles were renowned for their homemade cakes and ice cream.

More important than ice cream and cake, however, was the extraordinary devotion Daisy Ellington felt for her only child. (She would have a daughter, Ruth, when Duke was nineteen.) It must be said that the relationship between Duke and his mother was unusual. Duke later admitted that he was "pampered, and spoiled rotten," as he grew up. Daisy hardly let Duke out of her sight until he was four or five. Once when he was ill she sent for two doctors, and would have sent for more if she could have. When he was finally old enough to go to school, she would sneak along behind him, watching out for him until he got inside the school building, and frequently she would meet him after school and walk him home. Again and again she told him that he was special, that he was "blessed."

J.E., too, did the best he could for his family. As Duke said later, J.E. was the kind of man who lived like a millionaire, even when he had only a couple of dollars in his pockets. He dressed well, and he liked to own the best possible car. But with J.E. the family always came first. Nothing was too good for Duke's mother, so far as J.E. was concerned. He always got her the best.

Taken all together, Duke Ellington had in many ways a happier childhood than most Americans, black or white. Living in a relatively prosperous community, he was shielded from the worst effects of racism. He was doted on by his mother and was surrounded by a large family who pampered him. If money was at times tight, the family nonetheless was not in any sense poor. J.E., however much he enjoyed his good times, did not let them interfere with seeing that his family was properly supported.

This upbringing had certain obvious effects on Duke Ellington. It gave him a sense of security that he was loved. It made him confident that he could achieve what he set out to do. It instilled in him a pride in himself and in his black heritage; he would never, ever, allow himself to feel inferior to anyone. Indeed, it went even further than that, for he grew up believing that he was, as his mother so often told him, special—that he was above others, a prince moving among ordinary mortals. And if his mother believed that he was this special, it was up to him to see that he never allowed himself to be treated as ordinary.

CHAPTER TWO

Duke's family and the solid social group he grew up in were important in giving him a base on which to build a career for himself. They were also responsible for his nickname, which was given to him by a friend when he was still a boy. He seemed, even then, to be a natural aristocrat, and the nickname, Duke, fit.

At first it appeared that Ellington might become an artist. He showed some talent at drawing when he was a boy, and eventually he would win a scholarship to a famous art school, Pratt Institute in Brooklyn, New York, although for reasons that will become clear, he never took it up. As a boy Duke was more interested in art than he was in music—he simply liked drawing things.

And it was not impossible for a black to aspire to be an artist. We must remember that the segregation of blacks in the United States was not absolute; the walls were, to some extent, porous. Most white colleges and universities admitted a few blacks from time to time; blacks occasionally got appointments to judgeships and government offices; and some black children did mingle with white ones. For example, William "Sonny" Greer, later to be Ellington's most famous drummer, went to an integrated school in Long Branch, New Jersey, in the early years of the twentieth century. A number of blacks from Duke's generation did in fact become well known as artists in the 1920s and after. It was a possibility for the young Duke.

But there was also the tug of music. J.E. sang and played the piano a little by ear. Daisy had studied the piano more thoroughly and would play religious music and semiclassical pieces for the family and for visitors, as was customary in that time before radio, when the record player was still a novelty. It is important for us to keep in mind that the music to be found in Duke's home when he was growing up was not "black music," in the modern sense. The blues, the work songs, the ring shouts of the sanctified churches, which southern blacks, especially those who lived in the small towns and villages of the countryside, were hearing, would not have been permitted in the Ellington home. At that time these black musical forms were considered very "low class" by people like the Ellingtons; it was only later that they would come to be seen as significant, and studied by professors at universities.

Duke, then, grew up hearing the same kind of music that middle-class Americans of any race were being exposed to— light classical pieces, operatic arias, sentimental songs and ballads, and religious pieces. He learned early what was supposed to be "the best" sort of music—the sort of music that people described as "serious music."

But the truth must be told that he did not much care for it. At one point Daisy hired a piano teacher for Duke. Her name was Marietta Clinkscales, and the name seemed so funny for a piano teacher that for years people thought Ellington was kidding them when he talked about her. But she was real.

Daisy had not thought of training Duke to become a professional musician. We do not know what her ambitions for her beloved son were, but she probably had it in mind for him to become a professional of some kind, like the professional blacks she had grown up with. She wanted Duke to study music, because studying "good" music was supposed at the time to be uplifting; the child who had instilled in him a love of good music, and art in general—the finer things, as they were often called—could never go wrong.

So Duke took lessons from Mrs. Clinkscales for many weeks, but he did not learn very much. Indeed, one time when all her pupils were supposed to play for their parents and friends at a recital, Ellington had learned so little that Mrs. Clinkscales had to play the top part of Duke's piece, while he played the bottom part. Duke simply was not interested in "the finer things." He would much rather have been out at the empty lot on the corner playing baseball. And in time Daisy let him give up his lessons. But the lessons, however little Duke learned, were important for what he would become, because when he did get interested in music later on, he naturally gravitated to the piano. And of course a pianist is more likely to start thinking in terms of composing than, say, a drummer or a trombonist, because a knowledge of harmony comes with learning the piano.

Ellington's interest in music began when he was about thirteen or so. At this age he was starting to become interested in girls, parties, and mixing socially. He realized that anybody who could play music, especially the piano, was likely to be popular and get invited to parties. Duke, with his sense that he was special, was sure he ought to be popular. According to his own story, around this time he was sick with a fairly mild illness, but had to stay home for a couple of weeks or so. He used the time to work out on the piano a couple of original songs—the first of thousands he would eventually write. One of these he called "What You Gonna Do When the Bed Breaks Down?"

This was not a jazz composition. At the time, jazz, which had been invented in New Orleans only a few years before, was not widely known around the United States. However, one of the most popular forms of music at the time was one of jazz's ancestors—ragtime. Ragtime had a tricky, exciting rhythm to it, but it was stiffer than the swinging jazz rhythm to come. "What You Gonna Do When the Bed Breaks Down?" was really ragtime.

Not long after Duke wrote this song, the seniors in his high school put on a dance in the school gym. Duke was still in the ninth grade, but he and a friend decided they could crash the seniors' party if they could pass Duke off as a pianist. So Duke's friend pushed his way into the party, and announced, "This is the Duke. If you ask him nicely, maybe he'll play for you."

Duke was led to the piano. He was still far from an accomplished pianist. In fact, the only tune he knew was "What You Gonna Do When the Bed Breaks Down?" But even then Duke had the confidence that he could somehow bring it off. It would always be part of Duke's character to take chances like that. Years later, when he was famous, he would sometimes come to the rehearsal for a concert with no new music prepared, confident that he could create something at the rehearsal that would get by. He had this attitude right from the beginning.

So he sat down at the piano and played "What You Gonna Do When the Bed Breaks Down?" It was a hit, and the audience cried for more. Of course he had no other tune to play. He did not let that bother him, however, but launched into the same tune again, and played it with such style that he got away with it.

That was the real beginning of Duke Ellington's musical career. He could see, clearly enough, that music was one way of making himself a bit of a star among his social group in school. He knew he could not depend solely on "What You Gonna Do When the Bed Breaks Down?" forever, and he began trying to work out other things to play.

Once again we see how Duke Ellington's personality shaped the kind of composer he became and the music he created. Most kids of Duke's age who wanted to improve their musical skills would have asked their parents for piano lessons. But that was not Duke's way; he was simply too proud to put himself under the authority of a teacher. He did not want anybody telling him how to go about things. So instead of getting a proper music teacher and putting in all those hours practicing scales and finger exercises as he probably should have, he went out looking for shortcuts. Surely, he figured, there must be a way to make music that sounded good without having to go through those dreary exercises hour after hour, day after day. For this was another part of Duke's character: He liked to enjoy himself more than he liked to work.

In the end, then, Duke's music school was not a conservatory, but Frank Holliday's poolroom, which happened to be next door to the Howard Theatre, one of the most famous black theaters in the United States. At that time a theater like the Howard was not like the theaters of today which mainly show movies or plays. In those days theaters mostly offered "variety" bills made up of all sorts of different kinds of acts— dancers, singers, comedians, musicians.

Nor was Frank Holliday's poolroom like those of today. It

was more like a club, which attracted not only people interested in pool, but all sorts of people who wanted a place to hang out—lawyers as well as gamblers, champion pool shooters as well as youngsters like Ellington. And the entertainers from the Howard found it a convenient place for them to go between shows.

Among those entertainers were a number of very fine pianists. Some of them were technically brilliant and could sight-read anything. Others were mainly "ear" players who nonetheless had their own tricks and stunts.

Duke, inevitably, did not take formal lessons from these pianists. Instead, he would stand behind them as they played and watch their fingers to see how they got this or that effect, or played certain harmonies. When he got a chance he would ask them questions: How do you modulate from this key to that one, how do you play a good bass for such and such a tune? One pianist in particular took a liking to Duke. This was Oliver "Doc" Perry, a well-schooled pianist who carried himself with dignity and reserve and was respected by everybody. From time to time Doc Perry would ask Duke up to his house and show him things about piano playing.

Another pianist who helped Duke was Henry Grant, also a schooled musician. Grant was an important figure in Washington's black music circles. He taught music at the high school Duke attended, and he conducted choirs and orchestras. He, too, tried to help Duke improve his playing.

But despite the help of Henry Grant, Doc Perry, and the other players Ellington bumped into at Frank Holliday's, Duke was getting only a very haphazard musical training. The consequence was that he never, even long after he had become one of the most famous jazz musicians in the world, became a complete master of the piano. He could play wonderful jazz solos, and he was particularly admired for his "comping"—that is to say, his ability to accompany a band or a soloist with solid rhythm and interesting harmonies. But he never developed the brilliant technique possessed by such great jazz pianists as Art Tatum, Fats Waller, or James P. Johnson, all of whom were in Duke's generation.

Surprisingly enough, even though he came to be considered one of America's greatest composers, he never was a quick sight reader. As a youth, playing those parties and dances for friends around Washington, he could barely read music at all. Over the years, through experience, his reading improved, until he reached the point where he could read well enough to do what he had to do. But there were many ordinary pianists, wholly lacking in Duke's compositional genius, who could read music a lot better than he could.

This fact, too, proved important in Duke's development as a composer. Because he was not well trained technically, most of the time Duke had to work out his own method of doing things. If he did not know exactly how a certain piece was played, or a certain effect gotten, he would have to experiment at the piano until he found a way to get something close to it. In truth he was wasting a lot of time, for he was constantly "reinventing the wheel"—that is to say, putting a lot of effort into figuring out things which had been figured out by other pianists long before. But this method had significant consequences for him, because it forced him to find personal, and original ways of making music. Because no one was telling him, for example, that you do not put an E natural in an E flat chord, he might try the experiment, fooling around with it until he found a way to make it sound good. This method of working forced Duke to rely on his ear for almost everything. Because he did not know most of the rules, he had to depend upon his ear to tell him what was good or bad. Out of all of this came Duke's basic method of composition, which was simply to experiment on the piano, and later with the whole band, trying this and that until he found something his ear told him worked.

We should understand that a properly trained musician can sit down and work out a whole composition, especially if it is not a very complicated one, with paper and pencil, never touching the piano. Well-schooled musicians can look at a musical score and "hear" in their heads how the music will sound, just the way you can see in your head dancing snowflakes when you read the words "falling snow."

Duke eventually learned to work with pencil and paper to a greater extent than he had at first. But in the beginning he could not really hear how the music would sound by looking at the notation; he had to try it out on the piano in various ways until he hit upon what he liked. And in so doing, he was playing in a world without rules—or rather in a world in which the rules were set by Duke Ellington. Many people feel uncomfortable when they are set free to make their own rules; but for somebody like Duke, who saw himself as beyond other people, it was the only way to operate. It was part of his personality to hate rules if they were not his own. Years later drummer Sonny Greer, who became a close friend of Duke's, said, "Ellington would never ask you to show him something. No, his pride wouldn't allow that." Duke's pride, then, prevented him from acquiring a standard education in music; but in turn, it forced him to create a musical world for himself that today we can instantly recognize from a few notes as "Ellington."

Duke was still not a very good pianist, when at about fourteen he had an experience that pushed him to work harder. He was spending that summer with relatives in Asbury Park, New

Jersey. Somebody told him, "Man, in Philadelphia they've got a young piano player called Harvey Brooks. He's just about your age. You ought to hear him play. He's terrific." Duke of course was curious about Brooks, and on the way home from Asbury Park to Washington, he stopped off in Philadelphia with the person who had told him about Brooks. They went to hear Brooks. Duke said later, "He was swinging, and he had a tremendous left hand, and when I got home I had a real yearning to play." Harvey Brooks went on to become a competent professional musician, and made one record with the great Louis Armstrong. But he has never been numbered as one of the great pianists in jazz. Undoubtedly he impressed the inexperienced Ellington far more than he would a better-trained musician.

What seems to have excited Duke about Brook's playing was the swing to it. This was still not jazz, but ragtime; but Brooks was playing it with a lilt that Duke had not heard before, and was determined to incorporate into his own work.

In any case, by hook or crook, through his high school years, Duke gradually learned how to play the piano. And by the time he was sixteen or seventeen he was rehearsing with a group of fellow students in a local meeting place called True Reformer's Hall. Duke was not the leader of the group; instead, it was a loose-knit group without a leader. But from time to time they would be hired to play for school dances and the like.

It will come as a shock to young musicians today, who often find it difficult to get any kind of real work in music, that in those days there was such a demand for music that you did not have to be very good to get jobs, even fairly high-paying ones. The reason for this was quite simple: There was very little mechanical entertainment around competing with live entertainers.

It is worth saying something about this for a moment. Today

we are used to the sound of music coming at us all the time, via radio, records, tapes, discs, television, cable, and VCR. At the time Duke was in high school there was no radio or television. Records had been around for a decade or so, but both records and record players were expensive, and they were not in widespread use. In 1916 when Duke was rehearsing at True Reformer's Hall, the majority of American families had no way of reproducing music mechanically. If they wanted to hear music, it had to be live.

In fact, there was much less "canned" entertainment of any kind. Not only was there no television nor radio, but the movies were only at a beginning stage and were for the most part crude, brief films without sound or color. There were variety, or vaudeville, shows in theaters everywhere, but these shows were often too expensive for many people to go to very often. More often than not, people entertained themselves, and one of the things that they did most was to go out to dance in a cabaret, a restaurant, or one of the many thousands of dance halls that existed all over the United States at the time. Indeed, the period saw an enormous boom in dancing. Restaurants were forced to put in orchestras, so the diners could get up and dance while they were waiting for their food. People danced on the sidewalks in front of their offices at lunchtime, or in the aisles between the machines in their factories. It seemed as if everybody was dancing in every free moment they had.

Among other things, it was cheap for an organization or a club to put on a dance for its members. Many organizations, such as unions, fraternities, and the like, already had their own halls which were big enough for dances; and if they did not have a hall, it was not expensive to hire one. Then all you needed was a band, and if you didn't mind having your music fairly rough, you could hire a band of youngsters, like the ones rehearsing in True Reformer's Hall, for very little. A dance was a very inexpensive way for ordinary people to have a good time. That's why Ellington and his friends were able to get work, even before they had gotten very good.

CHAPTER THREE

If Duke Ellington had been born in another time and another place, he would probably have gone on to become a lawyer, a businessman, a politician, or other professional. He had been raised in a genteel home by parents who wanted the best for him. He was intelligent, talented, confident, good-looking and had the kind of manner and bearing that inspired respect. His parents had connections to the higher strata of Washington's black society, and there would have been no problem about his going to Howard University, had his school grades been good enough.

But a couple of things got in the way. One was Duke's resistance to lessons—to being taught. He never worked very hard at school, doing as little as he could and still pass, and spending his spare time enjoying himself, rather than concentrating on his homework. In the end he failed to graduate with his class. He had, we remember, won that scholarship to art school; but because he did not graduate from high school, he could not take up the scholarship.

A second problem was that he had fallen in love with a girl he knew around the neighborhood. Her name was Edna Thompson. In 1918, when Duke should have been making up the course he failed in order to get his high school diploma, he got married, and in March 1919 their son, Mercer, who would eventually assist Duke with the band, was born. Duke now had a family, and he had to find a way to make a living. In order to do so he opened a sign-painting business with one of the men in the little band he was working in.

But more and more he was coming to see music as the best road open to him. At about this time one of the top pianists from Frank Holliday's pool parlor asked Duke to substitute for him at a reception at a fancy country club near Washington. The pianist told Duke, "You're playing by yourself tonight. It'll be mostly atmosphere, just under-conversation music. Collect a hundred dollars and bring me ninety."

Duke was astonished. Ten dollars was a good night's pay for him and the young musicians he was working with at the time; and to think that the older pianist would have gotten a hundred dollars for the job. There was money in music.

By this time Duke realized that many of the big band leaders advertised in the yellow pages of the telephone book. These were mostly leaders who sent out several bands under their names each night and collected fees in the hundreds of dollars for each band. So Duke went to the telephone company offices and took out an ad that was bigger than those of the other leaders. And the work began to come in.

As ever in the music business, some funny incidents occurred. In one instance Ellington and his group were hired to play a barn dance. At the last minute the person in charge of the dance called Duke to say he'd just realized that the dance was to be on the second floor of the barn, and there was no way to get a piano up there. Duke said, "Don't worry about that, I also play guitar." The fact of the matter was that Duke did not really know how to play the guitar. But he sat there strumming it as if he did, while the other musicians played loud enough so that nobody would notice. It was typical of Ellington to see if he could get away with the stunt.

Duke Ellington, thus, was easing into the music business almost as a matter of chance. If he had passed one or two more classes, he would have graduated and perhaps gone on to study art. If he had not had a child when he did, he might not have been pressed for money, and perhaps would have gone back to school in order to graduate. So chance unquestionably played a role in making Duke a musician.

But there was another factor, which was that show business was one area of American life that was open to blacks. Going way back into the eighteenth century, whites had been interested in, or curious about, the music and dances they saw blacks doing in front of the plantation cabins, in their churches, in the corn and cotton fields, where they sang to relieve the monotony of hard labor. Many whites came to enjoy watching blacks sing and dance, play the drums and the banjo adapted from African instruments, or the flutes, fiddles, and trumpets they found in the United States. There was something different about these black dances and songs. They had a peculiar charm, many whites thought, and sometimes slave owners would bring parties of their friends out to the slave cabins to watch the blacks perform.

By the end of the eighteenth century slave owners were occasionally having talented blacks trained on instruments like the fiddle, the french horn, or the trumpet, to play for white dances in the parlors of the big plantation houses.

Then, around 1830, some white entertainers began doing

imitations of the music and dances of the plantation blacks. The most famous of these was a man called Thomas D. Rice. He happened to see an old black man, apparently crippled with arthritis, singing and dancing for his own amusement in a stable. The man sang, "Weel about and turn about and do jus so; Ebery time I weel about, I jump Jim Crow."

Rice was struck by the song and set about developing his own version of the dance. His act became spectacularly successful and led many other white performers to develop similar acts based on black song and dance. These performers "blacked up"—that is to say, darkened their faces with burnt cork or greasepaint, and put on comic versions of the clothes blacks were supposed to wear on the plantations. Needless to say, most of these acts were a good deal different from the real thing. They tended to be modified to suit white audiences—among other things, black plantation music contained deliberately off-pitch notes and counterrhythms which were unfamiliar to whites, and these were toned down. In addition, these acts aimed for laughs, and they usually portrayed blacks as lazy and stupid, although at times they presented a more sentimental version of black life in which the slaves were portrayed sympathetically.

In time whole shows of these white performers in blackface were put on. They were called minstrel shows, and they pretended to give their audiences a picture of the life of happy-go-lucky slaves on the plantations. In reality life for the slaves was not very funny nor filled with singing and dancing, although blacks frequently did sing while they worked. These minstrel shows became, through the middle decades of the nineteenth century, very popular with white audiences.

After the Civil War blacks were more free to travel and to start their own businesses than they had been. It occurred to some talented blacks to start their own minstrel shows—after all, they knew more about black folkways than whites did. These shows, however, were modeled after the white ones. Sometimes the blacks themselves "blacked up," in order to keep to the minstrel style, and they continued to present blacks as the grinning, shuffling ignoramuses of the white minstrel shows. These black show people knew better of course, but they felt that white audiences were not yet ready to accept a more serious, realistic view of plantation blacks.

Very quickly a few black entertainers began to make big names for themselves. Comedian Billy Kersands, who was also a song and dance man, was very popular with both white and black audiences. Composer James A. Bland wrote some of America's most enduring songs, including "Carry Me Back to Old Virginny," "Dem Golden Slippers," and "In the Evening By the Moonlight." By the turn of the century, black comic Ernest Hogan had become a star, and soon after, the team of Bert Williams and George Walker became one of the best known acts in the country. After Walker's death Williams went on to establish himself as one of the great entertainers of the twentieth century.

By this time minstrelsy had been replaced by vaudeville as the major form of American entertainment. These collections of a variety of acts were carefully arranged to provide contrast, and a swift pace, building to the headliner's "star turn." By the time Duke Ellington was born, vaudeville was a very big business indeed, netting millions of dollars for the big producers, and huge salaries for the top performers. To be in vaudeville in those days was as prestigious as being in a movie today.

Vaudeville, and show business in general, was open to blacks in a way that no other segment of American life was. Most vaudeville bills included a black act, and in the early years of the twentieth century some blacks were producing Broadway musicals written and performed entirely by blacks, for black and white audiences.

But for the most part, black comedians, dancers, and singers were still forced to present themselves as lazy ignoramuses who fought with razors, stole chickens, and ate watermelons. There were always some whites who appreciated blacks for what they were; but by and large, American audiences wanted to hold onto their picture of blacks as happy-go-lucky clowns. This tradition of the ever-grinning, clowning black entertainer would continue through most of the first half of the twentieth century, and even beyond. Such major black stars as Cab Calloway, Louis Armstrong, Eddie "Rochester" Anderson, Stepin Fetchit, and Fats Waller adhered to it. One of the people most responsible for bringing it to an end would be Duke Ellington.

One other factor that helped open show business doors for blacks was the belief that they had a special talent for song and dance. This idea was widely accepted by both whites and blacks. Indeed, the great black social theorist W.E.B. Du Bois believed that black and white souls were different in some respects. Blacks, according to Du Bois, were a "specially spiritual people—given especially to music, to color, and language."

What Du Bois meant was that blacks had a feeling for the arts in general, including painting, acting, and writing. Many whites were still not willing to go that far; they were not prepared to see a black actor play Hamlet, or a black vocalist sing opera. But there was widespread agreement that at least in the popular arts blacks had a special talent. They had "natural rhythm," or a "God-given gift for song." We are today less likely to think of blacks as having inborn skills of this kind; we are more likely to think that these things have to do with culture and training than with inheritance. But at the time Ellington was growing up, the belief that blacks had a special gift for music was widely accepted.

As a consequence, many black musicians were doing well for themselves. In New York, black bandleader James Reese Europe was providing much of the music for the most famous dance team in America, Vernon and Irene Castle, who were white. Other black bandleaders, like Ford Dabney and "Lucky" Roberts were being hired to work in the homes of the rich in New York and resorts like Palm Beach. The black composer Will Vodery was musical director for the famous Florenz Ziegfeld, a white man whose annual "Follies" on Broadway were among the most popular shows of the day. Another black composer, Will Marion Cook, had had several successful shows on Broadway. Others were writing hit songs for the music publishers of New York's Tin Pan Alley. Indeed, it had reached the point where many whites preferred to have black groups play for their parties and dances. Tom Whaley, later one of Ellington's assistants, said that during this period, "There was nothing but black musicians. White musicians didn't have a chance." This was something of an exaggeration, but it was certainly true that black musicians were welcomed in most places.

Thus, it was not merely chance that was pushing Duke Ellington in the music business; he was drifting there because that was where the current was flowing. Duke, as we have said, was never one to drive himself very hard except when he was forced to. He once said, "I never get anything done unless I'm faced with a deadline." It was not really in his personality to take a stand against Jim Crow, to struggle with the problems of segregation. As we shall see in more detail later, his way of dealing with the color line in America was to pretend that it wasn't there and simply walk through it. But given this attitude he was not likely to make a fight to get into a white university or join a white business firm. But a bit at a time, he drifted into the music business, and by the time he was twenty, he was more or less committed to it as a way to make his living. It is probable, at this early stage in his career, that if some great opportunity had come along in another field, he would have considered leaving music. He was not a man desperate to make music his life. But no such opportunity came along.

If Ellington was going to be in music, he would not be content simply to go along making a quiet living in Washington playing parties, dances, and receptions. If we know anything about him, it was that he was not going to settle for anything less than the big time. And in 1920 the big time, so far as show business went, was New York. There was Tin Pan Alley—the musical publishers who controlled the popular song market. There were the headquarters of the big record companies and the big vaudeville circuits. There were the famous nightclubs, restaurants, and cabarets which demanded a lot of music. To make a big success of yourself in the music business you had to be in New York. To young Ellington in Washington, New York seemed glamorous, wealthy, glittering, the town as bright as day at midnight, a place where nobody slept.

Particularly alluring was the black section, Harlem. There is not much glamorous about Harlem today. For decades it has seen much poverty. But in the years after 1910 and well into the 1920s, Harlem was a place of clean, spacious streets, pleasant homes, exciting night spots. Black intellectuals, poets, artists, were drawn to it. So were black doctors, lawyers, celebrated black show business people. So were gamblers and men who always seemed to have money, although they never worked. It was, in a sense, the black capital of America, the place all blacks wanted to see. By 1920 Duke was bound and determined he'd get there.

He was now part of a small group of musicians from Washington with whom he would be associated for some time to come. One of these was drummer Sonny Greer. Sonny was born William Alexander Greer in Long Branch, New Jersey. According to Sonny, his father was a master electrician for the Pennsylvania Railroad. His mother was a modiste—a fashionable dressmaker. Sonny had a confident and outgoing personality that helped him to charm people into doing things for him. He loved to play pool and practiced two hours a day, and it was his pool-playing skill which led him to become a drummer.

One day a black theatrical group, led by a well-known black songwriter and producer J. Rosamond Johnson, came to Long Branch. The show's drummer, Eugene "Peggy" Holland happened to like playing pool, and he came into the pool hall where Sonny usually practiced. He was impressed by Greer's skill and agreed to give Sonny some drum lessons, in exchange for some tips on pool playing. Sonny learned enough about drums to get into his high school band as a drummer, and by the time he was in his late teens he was gigging around his area of New Jersey. (A *gig* is a musician's term for a casual job.) This, in any case, was the way the story was told by Sonny, who was not always careful about the facts.

In time Sonny landed in Washington. His love of pool led him to Frank Holliday's, and there he met Duke and friends. He had developed a certain New York style of speech and had a smart line of patter which impressed the Washington musicians. He was in Holliday's one day when somebody rushed in saying that the drummer for the show at the Howard Theatre next door was missing and could anybody fill in? Sonny, with his natural confidence, grabbed the chance, and quickly became the house drummer for the theater. He was now part of the music scene in Washington and decided to stay there for awhile.

Sonny Greer was a showman by nature. He liked to flash his sticks around, and later on, when he was part of the Ellington band, he acquired an array of large gongs, cymbals, bells, and even kettledrums, which he could not play very well, but set up around himself in order to impress audiences. Years later Duke wrote a tune called "Ring Dem Bells." The arrangement of the tune required Sonny to hit a certain note on the gongs at given points. Sonny knew so little about playing the gongs that he didn't know which note he was supposed to hit, so he attached a little piece of paper to the right one. All went well, until one day some trickster in the band moved the paper to another note a half step away. When Sonny hit the note it sounded so terrible that the band could hardly play because they were about to burst into laughter. But Sonny just sat up there and grinned behind the drums, and went on hitting the wrong note right through the whole song.

Another musician who was part of the group was Otto Hardwick. Called Toby by everybody, Hardwick was a few years younger than Duke. But he was eager to join the musicians who were rehearsing at True Reformer's Hall, and he decided to learn the string bass. It was, however, a bulky instrument for a boy to carry, and he soon switched to the alto saxophone, which he would play throughout his career. Toby grew up to be a cheerful and irrepressible fellow, who frequently put good times before his duties as a musician, but he turned out to be an excellent player, especially of sentimental melodies.

A third musician who joined the loose-knit group at this time was trumpeter Arthur Whetsol. He was just the opposite of Toby Hardwick: a serious young man from a very religious family, who wanted to study medicine and thought of music as just a way to earn his college tuition. He approached music the way he approached everything else, with a great deal of seriousness. He studied properly, practiced, and developed a pure and accurate tone. He was one of the few good readers in the group, and he was also the one who would turn around and scowl at one of the others when he was not paying attention to the music.

One more young man who began playing around Washington with the others was Elmer Snowden, a banjoist. Snowden had been born and raised in Baltimore, where he became a professional musician as a teenager. Washington is only a short train ride from Baltimore. Snowden began coming over to Washington to play jobs there, and soon made that city his headquarters.

These young men, most barely out of their teens, and some still in them, were as much interested in good times as they were in music. They were all crazy about cars and bought the fanciest ones they could afford. Duke had a Chandler, and Toby one they called "the Dupadilly." They bought these cars used, many from a dealer they called "Dear Me." Toby's Dupadilly could only be started by coasting downhill. If it stalled going up a hill, everybody would have to get out and push it to the top so it could be started by coasting down the other side.

But if they did not always take their music as seriously as some musicians did, it was still their business. Little by little, working in various combinations and taking what jobs they could get, they established themselves on the Washington music circuit. They were not really a band, not really organized. But they were working in music.

CHAPTER FOUR

Duke Ellington did not like the term *jazz*. Once he became well established, he used to insist that he was writing "Negro music," or "the music of my people." Jazz, in the early days, had often been played in the dance halls and dives of the so-called vice districts which were a feature of most of America's big cities during the early part of the twentieth century. As a result, it was associated in the minds of many people with liquor, gambling, drugs, and vice. Duke had been raised in a respectable middle-class home by a mother who was in many ways quite puritanical. Jazz music was simply not acceptable to people of this kind, and that attitude stuck with Duke for the rest of his life.

But whatever Duke thought about it, his music has always been considered jazz by critics and musicologists, and Duke himself one of the leading figures in the music. This new hot music had been created in New Orleans around the turn of the century. Nobody is quite sure how it came about, but it is clear that jazz evolved from ragtime, one of the most popular musics of the time. It included elements of the blues, especially the bent "blue notes," and other ideas taken from marches, popular songs, and other sources. Crucial to it was the new, springy swing beat, much looser than the stiffer ragtime beat.

After about 1910 New Orleans musicians began to drift west and north, many of them landing in the vice districts of San Francisco and Chicago, where they introduced their hometown music to local musicians and dancers. (We must remember that in a day before radio and television, styles of entertainment spread more slowly than they do today.)

Then in 1917 a group called the Original Dixieland Jazz Band was brought from a Chicago dive to one of the fanciest restaurants in New York City. This was a sign that jazz was becoming respectable. The music quickly became popular, not merely in New York, but all around the United States, due to the best-selling records of the Original Dixieland Jazz Band. Soon young musicians everywhere were attempting to play the new music. Audiences began demanding it for their dances, their parties, and before long any good dance band had to be able to play at least a little jazz. Other good jazz bands came up from New Orleans to take advantage of the nationwide fad, and musicians elsewhere, as they learned how to play the music, organized bands of their own to play for dancing, and to make records. Not everybody liked jazz: many people continued to see it as a low-class music; others preferred the older ragtime, or the Tin Pan Alley hits. But in the years after 1917 jazz became increasingly popular across the United States.

Jazz music was brand-new, just beginning to become popular in the years that Duke, Sonny, Toby, and the others were getting into the music business. Although musicians everywhere were familiar with the Original Dixieland Jazz Band recordings, and possibly a few others, jazz playing was concentrated in Chicago, the West Coast, and of course New Orleans. There was not much live jazz in Washington around 1920 for Duke and his friends to study.

The kind of music people in Washington wanted at this period was straightforward dance music, with a little ragtime mixed in. And this was the kind of music that Duke and the rest were playing. Indeed, neither Arthur Whetsol nor Toby Hardwick ever became truly good jazz improvisers; they were known mainly for their ability to play pure, sweet melody. Duke himself at this time was more of a ragtime player than a jazz musician. Although we cannot be sure, these young Washington musicians probably added a few jazzy touches to their music. But mostly they were playing that fairly subdued "under-conversation music" that was called for at receptions and parties. At dances they would be required to play something with a firmer beat; but even so, it was not jazz.

Once again chance played a role in the development of Duke Ellington into the great jazz composer he became. By 1921 Duke and the loose-knit group of musicians around him had been playing professionally for several years. Sheer experience had helped to improve their playing considerably. Duke, although he was still using his various shortcut methods, was now able to sit down and rattle off a good many more tunes than "What You Gonna Do When the Bed Breaks Down?" They now had some confidence in their ability to please a crowd of dancers, or people at a party, and they decided that it was time to make an assault on New York.

But how were they to make contacts in that strange city? How were they to know who to talk to about jobs? They were considering the problem, and dreaming of the excitement of Harlem, when there came into the Howard Theatre a band led by a man named Wilbur Sweatman. He was no jazz musician, but a showman whose most famous stunt was to play three clarinets at once. However, he was trying to catch up to the new hot jazz which audiences were demanding, and he had worked out for his group some of the tunes that the Original Dixieland Jazz Band was making famous.

By chance, when he came into the Howard, he needed a drummer. Sonny Greer was available. Sonny insisted that his pals Toby and Duke also be hired. Sweatman agreed, and Toby joined the band. The band was soon to leave for New York, but now Duke was wary—he was making good money in Washington, and he wasn't sure he should give it up unless he had some sort of commitment of steady work. But in the end the lure of New York was too great, and he, too, went north, and joined the band when it was playing at the Lafayette Theatre in Harlem, another one of the famous black theaters.

The Washington men found New York as exciting and glamorous as they had expected. After their duties with Sweatman they wandered around Harlem visiting cabarets and after-hours clubs to listen to the great musicians who were gathering in Harlem. One place which particularly intrigued Duke was Mexico's. This was a small cellar club. Each night players on a given instrument were featured. One night would be trumpet night, another night saxophone night, and so forth. The musicians would engage in "cutting contests"—musical battles in which the players would try to outduel each other in their skill on their instruments and the brilliance of their musical ideas. Duke found tuba night especially fascinating, because there was not enough room in Mexico's for all the tuba players with their big instruments, so they would have to wait upstairs on the sidewalk until there was room for them. It was a peculiar sight to see a half-dozen tuba players gathered on a street corner.

Particularly impressive were the stride pianists like James

P. Johnson, Fats Waller, and Willie "the Lion" Smith, who had earned his nickname for courageous action in World War I. These stride pianists possessed brilliant techniques, and were the heroes of the Harlem music scene, far above the young novices from Washington. But their fame did not deter Sonny Greer from meeting them. He would walk up to one of them and say, "Hey, remember me? Sonny, the New Jersey kid?" The great man would assume that he'd met Sonny somewhere along the way, and get into a conversation, or even buy the Washington musicians a drink.

Unfortunately, after the Sweatman band's stint at the Lafayette was finished, the orchestra was due to go on tour. Duke, Sonny, and Toby could certainly have gone with it, but they were infected with the glamour of New York, and they decided to take a chance on staying, hoping that they could find a job playing somewhere—after all, a saxophone, drum, and piano made a natural combination.

They were optimistic. They had been good enough to play small dances and parties around Washington, but New York was the center of the entertainment business, and the city was filled with top quality musicians competing for work. So, although work was plentiful, fine musicians were in plentiful supply, too. They walked the streets by day and visited the night spots by night, hoping to find somebody who would buy them a sandwich, or at least a drink. Very quickly the money they had earned with Sweatman was exhausted. None of them were very good about saving money, especially Duke, who even when making millions later in his life never saved anything. One day, Duke said, they had to split a hot dog three ways—and he was only half-joking.

One man who tried to help them was Willie "the Lion" Smith. Smith was a confident man who loved to battle other musicians, as was the custom then. Most pianists who tangled with Willie the Lion were sorry they had, for he was a brilliant pianist. He would stand over the other player smoking a huge black cigar, and if the pianist had a weak left hand Smith would clench his teeth around his cigar and shout, "When did you break your left arm?" Soon enough the other pianist would give up and slink away. Then Willie the Lion would sit down at the piano and show how it should be played.

Willie the Lion took a liking to the Washington men and especially to Duke. He said, "I like you kids. You're nice clean kids and I want you to do well." He would buy them drinks and he once gave Duke money for a haircut so he could keep up his appearance.

This seems like a small matter, but it had important consequences. These three young men had come from proud families, with fathers and mothers who taught them good manners and insisted that they behave properly. They liked their good times, as young people always do, and as young boys they were capable of getting into mischief, like any other kids. But they had been raised not to be troublemakers, not to get involved in serious kinds of wrongdoing. They had too much self-respect for that. And this self-respect, combined with their decent behavior, communicated to the people they met. Like Willie the Lion, many people felt they were worthy of their help. Soon this would prove to be very important to them, and to what became of Duke Ellington.

But that time was not yet. One day Duke found fifteen dollars in the street. It was enough for three train tickets to Washington, and tired of scuffling, as musicians put it, they crept back home. But they had had a taste of the big time, and they were determined to get back there.

One person who had particularly impressed Ellington was Willie the Lion. Duke admired Smith's confident swagger and the flashy and exciting "stride" style he played, highly popular then, and still much used today. In stride the pianist's left hand hits a single note or octave, then leaps up the piano to play a chord on the next beat. The left hand thus appears to be "striding" around the piano. Meanwhile the right hand plays complicated, showy, and often very difficult figures which contrast sharply with the steadily striding left hand. There are others ways to play stride, but this is the basic scheme. Stride, in the hands of a master, develops a locomotive power and swing. Taken at top speed it is very difficult to play, and the best stride players were vastly admired by listeners, who expected to be astonished by the skill of people like Smith and his chief competitor of the day, James P. Johnson, considered by some to be the quintessential stride pianist. (One of the greatest of all stride pianists was Thomas "Fats" Waller, James P. Johnson's pupil, who became very popular in the 1930s. His records are easily available today.)

Duke Ellington had been aware of the stride style, and he knew that if he was to succeed as a pianist, he would have to become adept at it. He had managed to learn James P. Johnson's famous piece, "Carolina Shout," which all stride pianists felt they had to know, just to show that they could play it. Duke had learned the piece from a player piano. This was a very popular instrument of the time, which could automatically play tunes from precut piano rolls. The player piano could be slowed down, and the student could follow the keys as they were pressed down by the machinery. Duke had done this in order to learn "Carolina Shout," but it was not enough to be able to play just one piece. He would have to learn more.

But learning to play stride properly takes a lot of hard work—hours and hours of practice. Duke was looking for an easier method. As it happens, Willie "the Lion" Smith, although he was a master of stride, frequently used simpler types of bass for variety when he played stride, particularly the "walking" bass, in which the left hand walks a note at a time up or down the keys. This is a lot easier to manage than the standard stride pattern.

It appears then that Duke took Willie "the Lion" Smith for a model—insofar as he ever took anybody for a model—because Smith sometimes used simpler bass patterns which Duke could more easily imitate. Many years later he would write a piece in tribute to Smith, called "Portrait of the Lion." In time Duke did learn to play proper stride piano. But he was never one of the great masters of it and did not play it more than occasionally.

Although Toby, Sonny, and Duke had not succeeded at establishing themselves in New York, they had learned a few things from the experience. They had picked up some musical ideas, and they had got a sense of how things worked in the music business there.

Duke, in particular, was struck by the glamour of New York. He became a New Yorker in his heart from the time he first arrived there, and he continued to think of himself as a New Yorker even when he was away from the city on the road most of the time. Toward the end of his life, when New York was suffering from many problems, and no longer seemed as glamorous as it once had, Duke wrote a long paean to the city, saying "New York is a dream of a song, a feeling of aliveness, a rush and flow of vitality that pulses like the giant heartbeat of humanity." Many people would have said that by this time there were too many things wrong with New York to deserve that much praise, but Duke never got over his love for what became his city.

It is therefore not surprising that he wanted to get back there. But next time he would make sure there was a job waiting for him.

Back home the Washingtonians began scuffling for work again. Luckily, banjoist Elmer Snowden found the group a job in an Atlantic City club called the Music Box. The band consisted of Snowden, Greer, Hardwick, Whetsol, and Ellington. It was not an important job and it did not last long, but it was a stepping-stone in the career of Duke Ellington, for this was the group that would form the nucleus of the Ellington orchestra to come. In bands like this one, which do not work from written music, but some combination of improvised soloing and memorized parts, it is crucial that the members work together for a period of time, so as to put together a large enough repertory to get them through a night, and to see that all the pieces go smoothly. The job at the Music Box allowed them to do just this.

When the Atlantic City job was over they returned to Washington. And then luck intervened once again. Fats Waller, the young genius of the stride piano, was in Washington backing a vaudeville act. Waller remembered the Washington men from their New York visit, and they became reacquainted. When the vaudeville act returned to New York, Waller and some of the other musicians, bored with the job, quit. Fats recommended his Washington friends and wired them to come on up. This time J.E. gave Duke some money to get him through his first days in New York. But Duke as always, wanted to travel first-class. He bought a ticket for the parlor car instead of any ordinary coach, treated himself to a good meal in the dining car, and then took a cab, instead of a subway, from Pennsylvania Station up to Harlem where the job was supposed to be. He was then shocked to discover that there had been a mistake: The job had fallen through.

The Washington musicians were now right back where they had been the last time they had come to New York. However, they decided to stick it out as best they could. And once more their mannerly ways paid off.

What happened was this. Back in Washington they had gotten to know an entertainer named Ada Smith, who sometimes toured through that city. Smith would in later years become famous as Bricktop, the owner of a celebrated Paris nightclub. Now she was singing at a Harlem club called Barron's Exclusive Club. This was no ordinary dive. Barron Wilkins was well-known around Harlem, and his club was exactly what it said it was, exclusive. Men who patronized it had to wear suits and ties, women had to wear formal dresses. Barron's was a meeting ground for black artists and intellectuals. It also attracted wealthy black businessmen, athletes, and other black celebrities. When the club was first opened its clientele was mostly black. But this was a period when a number of whites, especially writers and artists, were becoming interested in black culture. Many of them were coming to Barron's to meet the black artists and intellectuals they found there. Barron's, according to Bricktop, "was *the* Harlem spot." And when she realized that these young men she had met in Washington were out of work in New York, she told Barron Wilkins that he ought to fire the band he was using and bring in the Washington musicians.

Bricktop must have known that these young players were by no means great musicians. There were, certainly, far better ones around New York at the time. But in a place like Barron's what mattered most was that the entertainers be well dressed and mannerly, and could be counted on to fit into the elegant atmosphere of the Exclusive Club. For Wilkins, maintaining the decorum of the place was more important than having a brilliant orchestra. Anyway, the music was supposed to be mainly a backdrop to the intellectual conversation that people came to Barron's for.

The job at Barron Wilkins's Exclusive Club was the break that the Washingtonians needed. Now they were being exposed to people who could do things for them, for among the people who gathered at Wilkins's were influential blacks, and whites from downtown who were up on the newest trends in things. A few months later, in the fall of 1923, a new nightclub called the Kentucky Club was opened in the heart of New York's famous Times Square entertainment district. (The club was called at first the Hollywood Club.) And the group from Barron's was chosen to provide the music.

The band was now called the Washingtonians. The official leader was banjoist Elmer Snowden, a situation that had carried over from the job at the Music Box in Atlantic City. (It is also true that Snowden was probably the best musician among them.) But in reality it was a cooperative band, with decisions made jointly by all five.

The Kentucky was by no means as exclusive as Barron's. For one, it was owned by a group of gangsters and managed by one of them, Leo Bernstein. It was not, in those days, surprising to find gangsters owning nightclubs. In 1920 the selling of alcohol had been made illegal all over the United States. Very quickly gangsters began making illegal alcohol or smuggling it in from Canada, Europe, or the Caribbean, and selling it undercover, often through hidden bars called speakeasies. Soon enough the gangsters began to take over the speakeasies and other places where alcoholic drinks were sold, and in time they came to control most of the nightclubs and cabarets in America's big cities.

Leo Bernstein and his pals were not interested in running a club for artists and intellectuals. They wanted a crowd of big spenders in the place—gamblers, entertainers, tourists on a spree to the big city, sports stars, and other gangsters. To collect this crowd they made the Kentucky Club into an after-hours place, which opened at eleven o'clock at night, and ran on until the last customer left, which was often after the sun was up. A place like this certainly did not call for polite under-conversation music. It called instead for the new hot music that was exciting young people everywhere—jazz.

Paradoxically, the Washingtonians were not really a jazz band, but a group specializing in soft, sweet music. But as we have seen, there was the idea around that blacks were by nature gifted at singing and dancing, and had a sense of rhythm that was inbred. This idea continues to be held to this day by some people. The truth of the matter is that scientists who have studied the psychology of rhythm carefully are not even sure what "a sense of rhythm" is, much less who has it.

But whatever the facts, it was assumed by Leo Bernstein and many of the customers who came to the Kentucky Club, that because the Washingtonians were black, they would be able to play hot music.

Ellington and the others did know something about jazz, even though they had not played a great deal of it. Once again chance intervened. In the summer before the band was due to open at the Kentucky Club, Arthur Whetsol decided he wanted to return to medical school. The band had been making a good deal of money at Wilkins's, mainly from tips, because the pay was low, and Whetsol had enough money for his tuition. So he left.

The group now needed a trumpet player, and sensibly, they chose one who could play the new hot jazz music. He was James Wesley Miley, always known as "Bubber." He had grown up in the San Juan Hill area of New York (near where Lincoln Center is now) at a time when it was filled with a lot of black clubs, and consequently a lot of music. Bubber turned to music almost instinctively. At first he was playing in the ordinary dance style popular when he was growing up. Then, when he was touring with a band through Chicago, he spent a few nights listening to the famous New Orleans cornetist, Joseph "King" Oliver. Oliver was a specialist in mutes, especially the plunger mute. The plunger was nothing more than the rubber cup at the end of a common plunger, the "plumber's friend" used to unclog toilets. By opening and closing the plunger over the bell of his cornet, Oliver could make all kinds of different sounds, varying it from moment to moment. At the time Oliver was considered the finest of all jazz cornetists, although he had in his band a man who would soon eclipse him—Louis Armstrong. Even today, King Oliver is considered by jazz critics to be one of the most important pioneers in the music.

Listening to Oliver, Miley grew very excited by the hot, swinging music the New Orleanian produced, and he determined to learn how to do it himself. He practiced hard. He also added a stunt of his own, which was to produce a growl in his throat while manipulating the plunger, to make his sound burn with an even fiercer fire. (We have to be careful about assigning credit for these various inventions. We cannot be sure that Oliver was the first jazz player to use mutes, nor was Miley the first to use throat tones to produce a growl.)

Bubber liked to tell stories with his horn. When he played his solo on a certain piece he would get a picture or an event in his mind and try to reproduce on his horn how he felt about the story. For example, for a piece of Duke's I will discuss shortly, called "East St. Louis Toodle-Oo," Bubber envisioned an old man coming home from his work in the fields to his dinner. The importance of Bubber Miley to Ellington—and to jazz history—was that he brought to the Washingtonians the true hot jazz quality it had lacked. He had a major effect on the

51

band's music very quickly. Duke said later, "Our band changed its character when Bubber came in. He used to growl all night long, playing gutbucket on his horn. That was when he decided to forget all about the sweet music."

CHAPTER FIVE

The Kentucky Club was an exciting place to work, filled with the sort of electricity Ellington had expected to find in New York. Though like all nightclubs outside of black districts it was for white patrons only, in reality the racial barrier was somewhat porous. Well-known blacks, such as the entertainers who worked in the Broadway area, or gangsters known to Bernstein and his pals could come in. Fats Waller and Willie the Lion would visit and sit in at the piano.

The club was in a small cellar. The ceiling was so low that the musicians could not stand erect on the bandstand, and it was impossible to play a string bass there. The bandstand itself was small, and Duke had to put his piano down on the floor.

There was other entertainment besides the Washingtonians. Usually the club had a rough show including a comedian, a dancer or two, and a chorus line of pretty girls. Sonny Greer sometimes sang with the band. According to Sonny, Leo Bernstein loved a song called "My Buddy," which was quite sentimental. According to Sonny, every time he sang it Bernstein would begin to cry, "and give the cash register away. . . . The money was flying."

As rough as the Kentucky Club was, it quickly became a center for entertainers who were working in Times Square and the Broadway area generally. Paul Whiteman, who had the most popular dance band in the country, would come in with some of his musicians. The great cornetist Bix Beiderbecke would come in. Actors, actresses, singers, and dancers—they'd all come into the Kentucky after their own jobs were over to kick up their heels. And inevitably, word about the Washingtonians began to get around show business.

The key figure, however, was not Duke Ellington, but Bubber Miley. His hot, growling cornet was featured on most numbers and dominated the band. Ellington was not yet composing many numbers. Much of what the band played were stock arrangements which could be bought at any music store. They might doctor these by adding introductions, solos, or changing them around in other ways, but in the main the excitement was provided by Bubber.

Working at the Kentucky was not all excitement; it had drawbacks. For one thing, the pay was low, and although tips were usually plentiful, they could not be counted on. For another, the gangsters were firmly in charge; the musicians could not argue about anything, but had to do what they were told. Among other things, Leo Bernstein laid the band off whenever it suited him. This particularly happened in the summer. This was a time before air-conditioning. A cellar club like the Kentucky would be like a steam bath on a hot New York summer's night, and it became the practice for Bernstein simply to close the club down during the hot months, making no provision for the band. The band would have to scuffle for whatever it could get. Luckily, the Shribman brothers, two promoters from the Boston area, took a liking to the band and frequently hired it to tour New England during the summers. But on the whole the Washingtonians were delighted to have the job at the Kentucky. They were now at the heart of New York show business.

By 1924 when the band had been at the Kentucky for a year, it was clear that the jazz boom was really on. Louis Armstrong had come to New York to play with the Fletcher Henderson Orchestra, and his brilliant solos were showing the New York musicians what hot playing was all about. The Henderson Orchestra was working at the Roseland Ballroom, a famous dance hall, and was growing into one of the country's finest hot bands. Clarence Williams was recording Armstrong and other budding jazz musicians in a series of recordings that would become classics, and Bix Beiderbecke and the Wolverines were making a name for themselves; they were in New York for a period at this time.

The Washingtonians began to see that they would have to expand their band to meet the competition. One of the first of the new additions was trombonist Charlie Irvis. He was a friend of Miley and had learned the growl and plunger style from him. He was a good choice, because the two of them could growl at one another. Now the growl style was central to the band's sound and it would remain so right to the end. Actually, Irvis did not remain with the band for long. He was replaced by trombonist Joe Nanton. Nanton became a master of the growl and plunger style, even today considered the finest trombonist ever to work in that manner in jazz. The other players called him "Tricky Sam." He would stay with Ellington until his death over twenty years later, providing an important ingredient to Ellington's music.

A more important addition to the orchestra, although he did

not stay for very long, was Sidney Bechet. Bechet was a New Orleanian, who was in on the new music from the beginning. He started as a clarinetist, but the soprano saxophone quickly became his main instrument, although he continued to play clarinet for most of his career. He had an enormous sense of swing, but played with a rich, flowing sound that overwhelmed the listener, and sometimes the other musicians in the band, too. He was one of the hottest players ever to come out of New Orleans.

Bechet was a loner, and a wanderer, who never stayed in one place for very long. Duke first heard him in a show at the Howard Theatre in Washington playing a solo on "I'm Coming, Virginia." He said later it was the greatest thing he'd ever heard in his life. Bechet had gone to Europe in 1919 with a group, but by 1924 he was back in the United States, living in New York and mainly playing casual gigs around the city—it suited his temperament not to stick with one job too long. Duke was eager to have him with the Washingtonians, and in the summer of 1924, when the band was making one of its annual swings through New England, they took Bechet along.

Bubber Miley had got the New Orleans style second hand from King Oliver, although he came to play it brilliantly, and Charlie Irvis had got it third hand from Miley. But Sidney Bechet was the real thing, a genuine bred-in-the-bone New Orleanian, who had been playing hot music from the time he was a boy. He and Bubber used to have cutting contests, smoking away at each other for chorus after chorus all night long. When he really got hot Bechet would "call Goola," his German shepherd. By this he meant that he would start growling away in the low register as if talking to a dog. Ellington said later that Bechet was "the foundation."

It was really Sidney Bechet and Bubber Miley who turned the Washingtonians into a jazz band. The other men got from them the New Orleans idea. It was an idea that was percolating through the American music world, and no doubt the Washingtonians would have in time come to it. But by 1924 they were listening to two masters of the style wail away night after night, and they began to understand how it was done. Then, early in 1924, there occurred a critical incident that changed not only Duke Ellington's life, but the course of American jazz. In the band business, as a general rule, a famous leader is paid a fee for each gig. Out of this money he pays his musicians, or "sidemen," as they are called, an agreed upon salary. Whatever money he has left after salaries and other expenses is his to keep. Big-name band leaders can become quite rich.

But with ordinary musical groups it is customary for promoters and club owners to pay so much per musician; in those days it might have been around fifty or seventy-five dollars a week, which was a good salary for the times. Usually the leader would be given something extra for his troubles. The point was that everybody in the band knew how much the club owner was paying.

One night at the Kentucky Club Sonny Greer went up to Leo Bernstein and said, "Man, when are you going to give us a raise?"

Bernstein was startled. "I just gave the band a raise," he said.

Now it was Sonny's turn to be startled. He went to the others, and they confronted Elmer Snowden. But Snowden had no explanation. Bernstein had given the band a raise, but Snowden had kept the extra money for himself.

That was the end for Elmer Snowden with the Washingtonians. Now they were without a leader. Not surprisingly, the choice fell upon Duke Ellington. He had always been "the Duke," a man whom the others admired and looked up to. But

57

there was also the fact that Ellington never liked taking second place to anybody. He liked being in charge of things, and no doubt he made it clear he would be happy to take on the job. At first being leader did not mean very much. It required Duke to collect the band's salary and pay the others off, to distribute the tips they received, and probably to decide what tunes they should play. But there can also be no doubt that Duke began, subtly, to turn himself into the real boss of the organization.

The catalyst was a man named Irving Mills. We need to understand that although there was a vogue for black entertainers, even the most famous of them were not completely accepted by many, if not most, whites. It was not always easy for a black musician to arrange meetings with record company bosses, theater owners, or club managers in order to sell themselves. They needed whites to manage them—to run interference for them and make contacts with the people who ran the music industry.

One group of people who fell into this role of providing management for black entertainers were Jews. They, too, had trouble being accepted by other Americans, many of whom saw them as strange people with foreign ways. It was therefore quite natural for blacks and Jews to form alliances in the entertainment industry. Jews frequently promoted black shows, opened nightclubs and dance halls to feature black entertainment—Leo Bernstein was one who did this when he opened the Kentucky Club—and to become bookers and agents for black talent.

One such man was Irving Mills, a short, flamboyant, sharply dressed man who had gotten into show business as a singer when he was still an adolescent. Eventually he and his brother Jack started a music publishing business. The business very quickly became successful. And by 1924 Mills Music was coming to be one of the major powers in the music industry.

In those days the big money in music was in the publishing of sheet music. Recordings were not nearly so important. But getting your song recorded was helpful in publicizing it. In order to get his songs out, Mills would sometimes organize and pay for recording sessions himself, and then persuade a record company to issue the record. To do this, he needed a band.

The Washingtonians had already made a few not very important records by the time Mills started to work with them, but once Mills began to use them the pace picked up.

Duke Ellington and Irving Mills seem like a very strange pair to be allied. Mills was shrewd, sharp, ruthless, and ready to cheat you if it seemed like a good idea. Ellington was a man with the sophisticated air, who always tried to appear to be above the common herd. But underneath Ellington was also a man who looked for shortcuts, who tried to make things seem to be more than they were. The two men respected each other, and became, if not close friends, at least allies.

Irving Mills has been accused by people of cheating Duke out of a lot of money. Among other things, he would put his name down as co-composer of many of Duke's songs, which cut him in on the money the songs earned. Many harsh things can be said of Irving Mills, and in the end Duke broke off the business relationship. But he remained friendly with Mills until the end of his life. Basically they saw that they could be useful to one another. Mills needed bands to do his bidding, and Duke needed somebody to promote the band.

In 1926 Ellington and Mills signed a legal agreement between them. Nobody today knows precisely what it said, but the result of the agreement was to change Ellington's relationship to the Washingtonians—Sonny, Toby, Bubber, and the rest. Irving Mills was the man who had access to the record companies, the publishing houses, theater managers, and club owners. He held the key which could open the entertainment industry to the group. And his deal was with Ellington, not with Toby, or Sonny, or Bubber.

Suddenly it was Ellington's band. The others could, of course, have quit, and formed their own group. But they did not; they accepted the new situation. For one thing, they saw clearly that they might have got along without Duke, for there were other good pianists around New York; but without somebody like Mills to front for them, they would go nowhere.

But there was more to it than that. The fact is that they all recognized that Duke Ellington was somebody special. He was not, perhaps, the best musician in the group: Bubber Miley was the player who excited audiences. But the others admired him just for being what he was: a strong-willed, intelligent man who would not humble himself to anyone.

Perhaps we should pause for a moment here and look back over the path Duke Ellington had trodden since the time when he painfully worked out at the piano his first song, "What You Gonna Do When the Bed Breaks Down?" We can see a number of fortuitous events along the trail. It had been Daisy Ellington, not Duke, who had initially decided he ought to play the piano. It had been a matter of luck that the Washington men had got the jobs with Wilbur Sweatman, and at Barron's. It had been a matter of chance that Irving Mills had decided to involve himself with the Washingtonians, rather than any of the many other bands working around New York.

But there was a lot more to it than chance. For at every turn in the road, Duke was making things go the way he wanted them to. It was not just accidental that older piano players like Henry Grant and Doc Perry went out of their ways to teach Duke some tricks on the piano; they did it because they found

Duke agreeable and personable, and his attention flattering to them. And they found Duke to be such a person because Duke wanted them to see him that way. In a similar way he saw to it that he would be at the center of his own social group, so that when bands were being formed, he would be part of them. He ingratiated himself with Willie "the Lion" Smith, Ada "Bricktop" Smith, and Irving Mills. He was not obvious about any of this. He did not fawn over people and tell them how wonderful they were. But he always seemed to be an easygoing, pleasant, well-mannered, well-dressed sort of fellow, who carried himself with a lot of self-respect.

Even after he became a great celebrity his style was not to shout at people and order them around. He always gave the impression that nothing bothered him, and he appeared to let his sidemen—the musicians—do what they wanted to. In fact, the Duke Ellington Orchestra, right from the first, was a very undisciplined group. Many of the men habitually turned up for jobs late, drank too much to play properly, or were rowdy on the bandstand. Duke always let it look as if he did not care what they did.

But the truth is that Ellington always knew what was going on around him, and he was always a lot more in control than he made things appear. Trumpeter Clark Terry, who played with Duke much later, said, "For all the seeming looseness of direction, Duke really runs things and, it seems to me, that his main goal as a leader is to mold a man so fully into the Ellington way of playing that he finds it hard to pull away." Other people who knew Duke well, including his son, Mercer, and his sister, Ruth, agree with this opinion of him.

It is therefore not surprising that once he found himself leader in place of Elmer Snowden, that he set about making it his band. Among other things, that meant shaping the music to his ideas. And if he was going to do that, he would have to start writing music. The trouble was, he really knew very little about music theory.

In 1924 Duke had discovered that anybody who wanted to could walk into a music publisher's office and attempt to sell them a song. Usually the publishers had somebody there who would listen to these songs and pass them along if he thought they were any good. Duke had hooked up with a songwriter named Jo Trent, and together they had written a few songs and managed to sell some of them. None of them were very important songs and did not make much money for Duke. But at least he had begun to compose a little.

However, sitting down at the piano and writing a song is relatively simple compared with working out a whole three-minute arrangement of a piece for a band. Another musician might have learned what he needed to know by attending a music school, or taking private lessons in music theory from a well-trained musician. But once again, Duke would not put himself under the tutelage of anyone. Instead, he did what he had done earlier when he was trying to learn how to play the piano, which was to get tips and hints from people who were well trained.

One of these men was Will Vodery, who was musical director for the famous Broadway producer, Florenz Ziegfeld. The other was Will Marion Cook, a symphonically trained violinist who had written several Broadway shows. Cook actually said to Duke, "You know you ought to go to the conservatory, but since you won't, I'll tell you. First you find the logical way, and when you find it, avoid it, and let your inner self break through and guide you. Don't try to be anybody else but yourself."

This was the sort of advice Duke was ready to take. Rules, he had always believed, were for others, not for him. Again and again through his composer career, when he was told about some musical rule he would immediately set about writing something that broke the rule.

Learning about music through haphazardly picking the brains of better trained men was hardly the best way to go about it. But it had always been Duke's way. And now, as he began to understand how compositions were put together, he started recording the first of the pieces that would make him famous.

The change in the band's style at this point is quite amazing, and very abrupt. Up until the late fall of 1926 the recordings made by the orchestra are quite ordinary and still fairly rough. Then, on November 29 the band went into the recording studios of Vocalion, a label which no longer exists, but which was quite well-known then, and produced several new pieces, among them "East St. Louis Toodle-Oo" (pronounced *toe-dul-oh*) and "Birmingham Breakdown." It is important for us to realize that these were not arrangements of previously written songs: They were instead complete jazz compositions, built around new melodies. Duke was not the first person to write whole jazz compositions; others had done it before, among them Jelly Roll Morton, who only a couple of months before this had cut several jazz classics, including "Black Bottom Stomp," and "The Chant." But most bands were recording arrangements of previously written songs; Duke, once again, was going his own way.

An analysis of "East St. Louis Toodle-Oo" can tell us something about Duke's compositional methods. In the summers, when the Kentucky Club was usually closed, the band was playing a lot of dances on the Shribman's circuit in New England. Bubber Miley had a habit of fitting music to words he happened to come upon. On the train from New York to Boston there was a sign for a cleaner called Lewando. As he passed it Bubber began to sing a slow, spooky melody in a minor key to the words, "Oh, lee-wando, oh lee-wando." Duke immediately pounced on Bubber's little melody and began to build a piece around it.

"East St. Louis Toodle-Oo" is mainly a feature for Bubber Miley, playing in his hot growl and plunger-mute style. It is mostly in the slow, spooky mood of the "Oh lee-wando" theme, but there are contrasting segments in major keys. Duke, was not, then, following the pattern of the sixteen or thirty-two measure format that was standard for popular songs of the time, but writing something more akin to a piece of classical music. Producing contrast through the shifting of keys, especially the movement from major to minor and back again had been used by composers of popular songs. The famous "Tiger Rag," one of the first jazz hits, moves through three keys, and the even more famous standard, "St. Louis Blues," written many years before 1926, features a movement from minor to major and back. But Duke's use of contrasting keys and themes was bolder and more dramatic than what was usually being done in the popular song format.

Duke did not work out "East St. Louis Toodle-Oo" by sitting down at his piano and painstakingly writing the piece out from beginning to end, as a trained composer would have done. That was not Duke's way; he wanted to hear how the various parts of the piece sounded as he was putting them together, and he obviously could not reproduce on the piano the sound of Bubber Miley's growls or Tricky Sam's plunger effects. Besides, at this point Duke did not really understand enough music theory to write out a piece like this in its entirety.

What he did instead was to bring the band into the recording studio, along with scraps of musical ideas he had sketched out on paper. Then he would sit at the piano, playing bits of melody and saying, "Bubber, you do this here, and saxophones, you back him up with this." Once he heard what it sounded like, he might change it, and go on changing it, until he got what he wanted. Then he'd go on to the next section. This would be Duke's main composing method for the rest of his life, although as time went on he would more and more work out his ideas on paper beforehand. But even at the end of his life he was still doing the bulk of his composing, not at the piano, but working with the band in the studio. As was said, Duke's real instrument was not the piano, but the band itself.

Working this way, it was inevitable that other members of the band would contribute to the process. Indeed, over the years they created a great deal of the music. Frequently Duke would give, let us say, the saxophones a melody, and expect them to work out the harmonies among themselves, which competent jazz musicians should be able to do fairly quickly. Often the musicians would contribute ideas for countermelodies, sometimes just to give themselves something to play while somebody else had the main melody. At other times a musician might suggest a way to improve a melody. And even after a tune was finished and recorded, both Ellington and the people in the band would offer suggestions for improvement. The drummer, the bass player, the guitarist, would almost always work out their own parts. Everybody put something into the pot; but Duke was the master who controlled it all.

One result of working this way was that most of Ellington's music, especially during the early times, did not get put down on paper. The musicians memorized it in the compositional process, although in some cases parts were sketched out as guides to memory. The advantage of this way of working was that when playing a piece, the musicians could concentrate on phrasing, dynamics, and the like, instead of reading the notes. The drawback was that when somebody new came into the band they were faced with figuring out for themselves what they were supposed to play.

Another result of Duke's manner of working was that the pieces never stayed the same. He was always thinking of ways of improving them. At times members of the band would add new things right in the middle of a dance or a concert.

It was not the usual way for a composer to work, but it suited Duke's personality. It left him free to test his own ideas according to his own feelings, instead of following the standard rules. And the final result was to give Duke Ellington's music a freshness, individuality, and uniqueness that no other jazz composer ever quite captured.

CHAPTER SIX

By 1927 Duke was firmly in charge of the Washingtonians, devising much of its music, and working out what jobs it would play and what records it would make with Irving Mills. No longer did the men in the band have much say over how things would be done. It was Duke Ellington's band, as we can see from the record labels. In 1925 the group was still recording as The Washingtonians. By the spring of 1926 it was Duke Ellington and his Washingtonians; in the fall it was Duke Ellington and his Kentucky Club Orchestra, and by the next year the name was simply Duke Ellington and his Orchestra. For a while Mills continued to record the band occasionally as the Washingtonians, when he wanted to record with a company other than the one the band was contracted to; and he used other names when it suited his convenience, some of them pretty strange, like The Whoopee Makers and The

Harlem Footwarmers. But in the main it was Duke Ellington and his Orchestra.

By this time the demand for black entertainment in the United States had grown to a full-scale boom. All-black shows were being mounted regularly on Broadway. Black dance bands, like that of Fletcher Henderson, were rising into popularity. Singers and dancers like Florence Mills and Bill "Bojangles" Robinson were national celebrities; when Florence Mills died suddenly at the peak of her fame her funeral was attended by thousands of people, both black and white. Duke wrote a piece in tribute to her, which he called "Black Beauty." The idea that blacks had a special talent for song, dance, and comedy was in full flower.

Given this interest in black entertainment, it occurred to some promoters to open nightclubs in Harlem, the black section of New York. By the mid-1920s there were a number of clubs there, most of them featuring jazz. Some of these clubs were intended primarily for blacks, although a few whites might come as well. Some were what were called "black and tans," which meant that they were racially mixed. Others—and these were usually the fanciest and most expensive of the clubs—were open to whites only.

The most famous of these was the Cotton Club. Indeed, it is still the most famous of American nightclubs, even though it was closed over fifty years ago. Many entertainers who went on to become famous got their start at the Cotton Club, among them Lena Horne, Cab Calloway, Ethel Waters, and Duke Ellington. The Cotton Club has been written about many times in books and magazines; there has even been a movie about it.

The Cotton Club was started by a gangster named Owney Madden, who had murdered several people before he was twenty. Nonetheless, the Cotton Club was a very fancy place with an elaborate show. It was decorated to look like a cotton plantation, but there were also palm trees around, which were supposed to suggest the jungle. There were two shows a night, which were almost as complete as Broadway shows and would last for an hour or longer. In between the shows the orchestra would play for dancing.

The Cotton Club attracted the rich and famous. The mayor of New York, Jimmy Walker, often came. So did sports celebrities like Babe Ruth, the great home run hitter. Of course show business people were always there—movie stars, actors and actresses, famous band leaders. On Sunday night entertainers were often asked up onto the stage to perform one of their specialties. Inevitably, the Cotton Club was a magnet for tourists, if they had plenty of money to spend. Although the Cotton Club was supposed to be segregated, which was legal in those days, blacks were allowed in if they were well-known show business people.

The entertainment was all black, although some of the people behind the scenes, like songwriters Jimmy McHugh and Harold Arlen, were white. The Cotton Club was a very prestigious place for a black entertainer to work, and many of them were eager to get jobs there, even though the pay was not very good. In 1927 the Duke Ellington Orchestra was really not quite good enough for the Cotton Club. Many of the musicians read music very badly, some were not well trained, and Duke himself was still only beginning to learn how to compose. But chance took over.

What happened was this: In the fall of 1927 the orchestra was once more out of the Kentucky Club and working at a theater in Philadelphia. At that moment the Cotton Club decided to change bands. The management offered the job to

King Oliver, the cornetist who had inspired Bubber Miley. But the Cotton Club was noted for paying low salaries, and Oliver turned the job down.

Then Ellington's name came up for consideration—after all, he had been at the Kentucky Club in the heart of Broadway for four years, off and on, and anybody who was interested in New York nightlife would know about his band. Irving Mills quickly phoned Ellington at the Philadelphia theater and told him to bring the band to New York for an audition the next day at noon. The problem was that the Cotton Club wanted an orchestra a little bigger than Duke's was. Over the past few years a number of musicians had been with the band for brief periods or had joined it for recording sessions, and would know some of the repertory. Duke set about rounding up two or three extra players. This took a few hours, and by the time he managed to get his band to the club it was two in the afternoon. Fortunately, Owney Madden's partner, who was supposed to decide which band to take, also arrived late. He heard the Ellington group, liked it, and hired it on the spot.

So, in any case, was Duke's story. But Duke liked to tell stories of this kind, to show how casually he operated, and undoubtedly there was more to it than that. The key must have been Bubber Miley. After all, the club had originally wanted Bubber's mentor, King Oliver; surely it made sense to get a band with a player in the Oliver mold. It was, then, the growl and plunger style that got the Ellington band the job at the Cotton Club.

The Ellington men were overjoyed to be going into a club which was far more important than the small, grimy cellar club they had been working in. But there was one more problem: They were still under contract to the theater in Philadelphia. According to the story, Owney Madden got in touch with a gangster he knew in Philadelphia. The gangster went around to see the theater owner. "Be big," he told the owner. "Or you'll be dead." The theater owner released Duke from the contract.

The fact of the matter, however, was that the Duke Ellington Orchestra was not really up to playing the Cotton Club job. For one thing, singers and dancers often brought with them their own arrangements of the music they wanted to back their acts. Most of Ellington's men did not read well, and it would be a struggle for them to learn to read a lot of new music. For another, Duke was expected to produce a steady stream of arrangements of new tunes—popular tunes of the day, and the special songs the Cotton Club's own songwriters turned out. Once again, Duke was by no means a deft and quick arranger.

But Duke was determined to make a success of the Cotton Club job. It was a wonderful opportunity for him and his musicians, and he meant to make it work. One break was that each Cotton Club show ran for six months at a stretch; once the show was worked out the band could coast for awhile and try to polish the pieces they played every night.

In order to give the band a distinction and individuality, Duke and Irving Mills worked out the idea of building the music around what they called the "jungle sound." In part this grew out of the animallike growling of Bubber and Tricky Sam. In part it was supposed to fit in with the jungle theme that the club featured, based on the idea that blacks were somehow connected to the jungle. This was not only insulting to blacks, but simple nonsense. Most blacks came from families who had been in the United States for a hundred, two hundred, or even three hundred years. Furthermore, many of the tribal groups from which American blacks are descended had not lived in wooded areas at all, but on grassy plains called savannahs.

Certainly the suave Duke Ellington had grown up in an environment that was far removed from the jungle. His sister,

Ruth, once remembered sitting in the family's Washington home waiting to hear the broadcast from the Cotton Club. Suddenly the announcer came on and introduced "Duke Ellington and his Jungle Music." Ruth said:

> It was quite a shock. Here we were, my mother and I, sitting in this very respectable Victorian living room in Washington, my mother so puritanical she didn't wear lipstick and the announcer from New York telling us we are listening to Duke Ellington and his Jungle Music. It sounded very strange and dissonant to us.

But if the idea of Jungle Music was not very logical, it was a good commercial gimmick to help sell the band. So it stuck, at least for awhile, until it was no longer needed. Indeed, sometimes the orchestra even recorded as the Jungle Band.

Duke now set out to build up the band's repertory. It already had some good pieces like "East St. Louis Toodle-Oo" and "The Mooch." But the band needed more. Now Ellington's ability to improvise something that sounded good out of bits and pieces of musical ideas proved to be valuable. Following his usual method, he would bring the band into the club in the late afternoon, and feed it new arrangements from the piano, a few notes at a time. He leaned heavily on his improvising soloists, especially Bubber Miley, because solos help to fill out numbers, saving a lot of rehearsal time. In many instances Duke only worked out an introduction and an opening chorus, and then turned it over to the soloists. To give the effect that there was more happening than there actually was, he might insert between solos a brief interlude, perhaps changing the key. Then he would repeat the opening chorus at the end to round the piece off. Frequently the other musicians would work out backgrounds to play behind the soloists. In this way Ellington could stretch two or three melodic ideas in a full three-minute piece.

But other pieces were more fully worked out. And the pieces grew over time as the musicians, or Duke, thought of new things to add.

Duke also began reaching out for new musicians who he thought could contribute to the band's sound. In the past decisions about new members had been worked out mutually. In other instances, especially when the band was recording, Mills would insist on bringing in extra musicians for the date who were good readers and could be expected to do a good job quickly. But now it was Duke's band, and he would make choices, although he listened to advice offered to him by the other men about musicians they may have heard one place or another. As we shall see in a moment, the type of men Duke chose says a good deal about his attitude toward his music.

One of the first of the men he brought in was clarinetist Barney Bigard. He was a New Orleanian and had grown up hearing jazz first hand. As a result, he was a step ahead of the New York musicians. Furthermore, he had had better training than some of the other men.

Duke heard Barney playing at Mexico's. He was particularly impressed by Bigard's "liquid" or "woody" tone. He asked Bigard to come and see him. Barney said later:

> I noticed he kept talking in the plural . . . "Our band." "We can stay there," and I liked that from the start about him. He thought of a band as a unit, and I dug him.

Bigard was convinced and joined the band at the beginning of 1928, when Duke had been at the Cotton Club for a month or so. He would stay with the band for some fifteen years. The liquid quality of his clarinet playing long runs up and down the

73

scale would become an important part of the band's sound.

A second major addition to the band in the early days at the Cotton Club was Johnny Hodges, known to everybody as Rabbit, or Rab. He got this nickname, Hodges said, because as a boy he was fast on his feet.

Johnny Hodges was born and raised in Boston. He grew up knowing two other youngsters who would also become important jazz saxophonists, Harry Carney, who joined Duke soon after Hodges, and Charlie Holmes, who became the featured saxophonist with the great Louis Armstrong's orchestra.

Like young people all around the United States, Hodges and his friends fell in love with the new jazz music sweeping the country when they were teenagers. Hodges liked the way saxophones looked, and he eventually acquired a soprano saxophone. He soon heard about the master of this instrument, the New Orleanian Sidney Bechet. In 1924 Bechet was traveling with Jimmy Cooper's Black and White Revue, which featured black entertainers for the first half of the show, and white entertainers for the second half when the show came to Boston.

Bechet knew Johnny Hodges's sister, who told him that her younger brother was a great fan of his. Bechet told her to bring Johnny around to his dressing room after the show. Hodges arrived carrying his saxophone in a sleeve cut off from a coat. He played a popular tune of the day called "My Honey's Lovin' Arms" for Bechet. Sidney could see that Johnny had talent and showed him a few things about saxophone playing. For the rest of his life Johnny Hodges would be a devoted fan of Sidney Bechet, and did his best to acquire Bechet's style.

Hodges began coming to New York whenever he could. He would spend his time following Bechet around from one club to the next, sometimes sitting in. Eventually Bechet hired him to work as a duet with him in a New York club. The job did not last very long—Bechet was footloose and never stayed in one place very long—but it was a wonderful training experience for Hodges.

Duke Ellington first heard Hodges playing alto saxophone in a Boston club, on one of those summer swings around New England. Given his love for Bechet's playing, Duke was eager to get somebody who could play like Bechet for his orchestra. But Hodges was shy, and he wouldn't join the band. Over the next few years he was back and forth between New York and Boston. Finally, not long after the Cotton Club opening, Otto Hardwick was injured in an automobile accident, and Duke persuaded Hodges to join. Hodges went on to become the finest jazz alto saxophonist of his time. He possessed a rich, honey-like tone that poured like heavy cream, and he played with an immense swing. He never became a very good reader, and even after he had been with the band for years would have to be coached in his part by the other saxophonists. But he was such an exciting player that nobody minded this. Hodges was best known for his alto saxophone work, but he continued to play soprano for many years; the influence of Bechet was always evident in his playing. Even though Duke had not been able to keep Sidney Bechet, he had found somebody who was nearly as good on soprano, and who was also one of the great masters of the alto saxophone.

As I have said, in the past there had been some tendency to add to the band musicians who were good technicians, good sight readers and *executers* as the term was, who could play with speed and good tone.

But that was not Duke's idea. As we have seen, Duke did not grow up surrounded by jazz, as the New Orleanians had, and when he was gigging around Washington he was not essentially a jazz player. But by the time the band had reached the Cotton Club, he had come to understand what jazz was all about—that the essence of it was rhythmic swing, drive, passion. It was these things he wanted from his musicians. They could learn to read and to get around rapidly on their instruments. But nobody could teach a musician how to swing, how to play with feeling. Especially, nobody could teach a player that individuality which is so crucial to jazz playing—that ability to "tell your own story," as the musicians put it. That had to come from inside, and so the musicians Duke chose would first and foremost be fine jazz improvisers. He reached out for people like Hodges and Bigard, who could play with fire.

Duke was building his band around the musicians, rather than around a particular style of music, or certain types of effects, as most band leaders did. For example, the Glenn Miller Orchestra, which would become one of the most famous of the swing bands a few years later, was built around certain devices, like having the clarinet play the lead over the saxophones, which gave the sax section a particular quality that listeners would always identify as the Glenn Miller sound. For Miller it did not much matter which musicians he had in the band, so long as they could read quickly and play well.

But to Duke it did matter who the musicians were. It was a wise theory, for in the end he had musicians who could not only play the arrangements with verve and swing, but who were also among the most brilliant soloists in jazz.

And so, one at a time, Duke brought them in: Harry Carney, who would anchor the saxophone section with his baritone saxophone and make that cumbersome instrument swing; Juan Tizol, a dazzling technician on the valve trombone, who played with a pure, sweet tone; and others, among whom was the old Washingtonian Arthur Whetsol, who finally decided to give up medical school and make his life in music.

But if Duke could hire, he could also fire. Without doubt,

despite the new talent Duke had added to the band, the crucial person was Bubber Miley, who along with Tricky Sam provided the jungle sound. But unfortunately, Bubber was growing increasingly unreliable. The main problem was liquor. After playing at the Cotton Club all evening he would often go out on the town, running from a party to an after-hours club and more parties. He would then turn up for the job not only drunk, but exhausted from staying up all night. He might still be wearing his band uniform from the night before, by now stained with spilled food and liquor. He even took to keeping some talcum powder in his trumpet case to sprinkle on the food stains. When he turned up like this the other members of the orchestra would let him sleep between sets, and by the end of the evening he would be rested and playing well. But then he would do it all over again.

This was bad enough; but sometimes Bubber made things even worse by not showing up at all. There was one famous occasion when the band was to record its first great hit, "Black and Tan Fantasy," when Bubber did not appear, and another trumpeter had to be hastily sent for to play his part. Many nights he would not get to the Cotton Club until after the band had started, and sometimes he would never get there at all. Duke hated to fire Bubber. He was always very loyal to his men, and would stick with troublemakers long after other leaders would have fired them. But what was the use of being loyal to Bubber, when he wasn't doing the job? And so, reluctantly, in 1929 Duke had to fire Bubber Miley.

It was all too bad. For the Duke Ellington Orchestra was climbing to fame and glory, and it would leave Bubber behind. If only he had been able to curb his appetite for liquor and all-night parties he might have become one of the great stars of the swing band era. But it was already too late for Bubber; he drifted around the edges of jazz for two or three years, and then died of the effects of alcoholism.

The man who Duke picked to replace Bubber Miley was a typical Ellington choice. His name was Melvin Williams, but he was always called Cootie, a nickname he had picked up in childhood. He was born in Mobile, Alabama. His mother died when he was young, and he was raised by his father and an aunt. Cootie's father was a remarkable man. He was so big and strong that at one point somebody wanted to train him to become a heavyweight boxer. For awhile he owned a gambling hall, making a lot of money which he spent at the racetrack. But in time he gave up the fast life and became a minister.

Whatever kind of life he led, he was always a good father. He was concerned about his children and was stern with them. Among other things, he insisted that they all learn to play music. He would not let them just pick up an instrument and teach themselves, as many young musicians did, but required them to study with proper music teachers.

So Cootie studied what musicians of the time called "legit," learning a "legitimate" technique of the type a bandsman or symphonic musician would acquire. This proper course of study gave him a solid foundation. He became an excellent reader, and possessed an accurate and powerful sound.

But the young Cootie Williams was really more interested in playing jazz than in practicing the exercises in his book. His teacher would smack his knuckles when he played jazz, but Cootie wouldn't give it up. At the time he was going through his teens the great New Orleanian trumpeter Louis Armstrong was making his classic Hot Five series of records, which struck the jazz world with the force of a sledgehammer. Cootie studied all of Armstrong's records and learned to play many of Louis's famous solos. He very quickly became a fine jazz improviser, with the influence of Armstrong evident in his playing for the rest of his life.

In hiring Cootie Williams, Duke was once again showing his determination to have the finest of jazz players in his orchestra. And again he had reached out for the New Orleans sound. Ellington now had his clarinet soloist the New Orleanian Barney Bigard. His primary saxophone soloist, Johnny Hodges, had formed his style on that of the New Orleanian Sidney Bechet; and his main trumpet soloist, Cootie, was a devotee of another New Orleanian, Louis Armstrong.

Like Johnny Hodges, Cootie Williams went on to be one of the premier jazz soloists of his day, and eventually a star in his own right. His story makes a pleasant contrast to that of the hapless Bubber Miley. Bubber could not discipline himself, and did not take enough pride in his work to want to play as well as he could—good times meant more to him. Cootie Williams, on the other hand, was a disciplined, hardworking, proud man, who often cracked down on the other musicians when they weren't taking the music as seriously as Cootie thought they should. And in the end it was Cootie's version of the growl style Bubber had developed that became famous.

But we must respect Bubber Miley's contribution to jazz, for he was one of the major forces that put the Duke Ellington Orchestra on the road to fame.

CHAPTER SEVEN

The years at the Cotton Club were very exciting ones for Duke and the musicians in the band. They were mingling with all kinds of people: movie stars, gangsters, artists, politicians, intellectuals. As members of the orchestra at America's most famous nightclub they were stars themselves. They were invited to parties, taken out for dinners, given free meals at restaurants. And there was always the joy they took in playing their own type of music. It seemed, at that moment, as if they were at a party which would go on forever.

One very important factor in helping the band along was the arrival of network radio. (There was no television at this time.) Radio was young. The first true broadcast had been made only seven years before Duke opened at the Cotton Club. At first all radio stations were local, broadcasting only to their own cities and the surrounding area—although in fact some of the more powerful stations could be heard for long distances. But by

1926 people were starting to put together combinations, or "chains" as they were sometimes called, of radio stations linked across the country. The two most successful of these radio chains were the Columbia Broadcasting System and the National Broadcasting Company, the famous CBS and NBC of today.

Suddenly it was possible for a broadcast to be heard everywhere in the country at once. But what kind of programs should be sent out over the air? One obvious answer was music, and in the early days of radio, music was the basic staple of radio broadcasting.

Nor was it recorded music. The idea of the disc jockey spinning records had not been widely accepted. Radio stations hired orchestras, sometimes quite large ones, to broadcast regularly from their studios. But they also found that it was a simpler matter to take a microphone into a nightclub or dance hall where a band was playing, and broadcast directly from there.

Luckily for Duke, his band had acquired a fan named Ted Husing, who had done some local broadcasts of the group from the Kentucky Club. Husing suggested to the new Columbia Broadcasting System that it do some broadcasts from the Cotton Club. He was sure that Americans out in the hinterlands would find it very exciting to hear live broadcasts from this famous nightclub, populated by gangsters, movie stars, and other big names.

To the Cotton Club audiences the Ellington Orchestra was only part of a show that included dancers, comedians, and other acts. But dancers were not much use on a radio broadcast, and neither were most comedians, who often depended on gestures and facial expressions to get their laughs. Inevitably, the radio broadcasts from the Cotton Club featured the band. Ted Husing would announce "From the Cotton Club,

Duke Ellington and his famous orchestra," and the band would swing into one of its great numbers like "Mood Indigo," "Black and Tan Fantasy," or "Ring Dem Bells." All across America people would dance to the music in their living rooms, or just sit back and listen, imagining that they were in the Cotton Club mingling with celebrities. Ellington's music, and his name, were being spread across the country.

But radio was not the only factor that was pushing Duke Ellington into celebrity. Just as important was a sweeping change taking place in American society—in the way Americans thought and felt about things. There was a feeling in the air in the 1920s that a new age had arrived—what came to be called "modern times." New forms of art, like cubist painting and atonal music, were pushing aside the old ones. New dances, faster and less decorous, were replacing the polite dances of the Victorian age. Skyscrapers were rising in American cities, airplanes were appearing in the sky, and cheap new, mass-produced automobiles, hitherto a rich man's toy, were being bought by ordinary people.

In the 1920s jazz was seen as part of the new spirit, something that came along with airplanes, cubist paintings, skyscrapers, and the fast new dances. It was the theme music of the new age, so much so that very early in the 1920s the famous novelist F. Scott Fitzgerald termed the period the Jazz Age.

Jazz was seen by many not merely as a music to be danced to, but a new type of art that had to be taken seriously. And through the last years of the 1920s and the early 1930s, Duke Ellington was more and more taken to be the leading figure in jazz.

The musicians themselves, and close fans of jazz, would not necessarily have agreed. Duke Ellington had his supporters among these people, of course, but some tended to think that the great improvisers, especially Louis Armstrong, Bix Beiderbecke, Jelly Roll Morton, and some others were the great heroes of the music. Others felt that only the New Orleans jazz of King Oliver's Creole Jazz Band, and similar groups, was the real stuff. These people were inclined to think that Ellington's music was too sophisticated, not earthy enough, to be good jazz. So there was disagreement in the jazz world about Ellington's music.

But to intellectuals, artists, and music critics, the Ellington Orchestra was at the forefront of jazz. Duke Ellington, to them, was not merely an improviser, but a composer. He was, they felt, a *modernist,* using many of the devices employed by such great innovators as Claude Debussy, and Igor Stravinsky, two great stars of modern music. Indeed, many music critics were sure that Duke must have made a deep study of modern music. One of them, R. D. Darrell, called Ellington a genius, and wrote:

> The most striking characteristic of all his works, and the one which stamps them ineradicably as his own, in the individuality and unity of style that welds composition, orchestration, and performance into one inseparable whole. . . . His command of color contrast and blend approaches at times an art of polytimbres.

Darrell, and other intellectuals, were taking Duke Ellington seriously indeed as not a mere dance band leader, but as an artist, as important in his own way as Debussy, the new novelists like Ernest Hemingway, the fauve and cubist painters like Matisse and Picasso.

As a matter of fact, Duke was not really aware of the attention he was getting from the music critics and the intellectuals in general. He was always more interested in the immediate things around him— the piece that he was working on, the meal he was about to eat, the men and women he was talking to at the party he was attending. But in time it would have an effect on him.

Despite all of this, keep in mind that, while radio and the spirit of the Jazz Age were helpful in making Duke famous, the key matter was the music itself. People were attracted to it— music critics, many jazz fans, and millions of ordinary people who liked to dance to it. What was it about Duke's music that commanded the attention of so many different kinds of people?

The primary ingredient in jazz has always been its special rhythm—that springy "swing" which seems to uplift the listener. The music of Duke Ellington had that quality. A lot of the band's swing was provided by those people, like Hodges and Williams, who were under the influence of the New Orleanians; but by the late 1920s the Washingtonians had learned how to swing, too.

However, many jazz bands could swing, and there were those who believed that some other groups, like Duke's chief rival Fletcher Henderson, could swing harder than the Ellington Orchestra.

But Ellington's music had certain qualities that eluded many other jazz groups. One was that R. D. Darrell called Duke's "command of color contrast and blend." Duke, as a boy, had been interested in painting, and even later in life he would pick up the paintbrush in those rare moments when he had a little spare time. He had a sense of color, and not surprisingly he tended to approach music somewhat as a painter might approach a canvas. That is to say, he used the sounds of the musicians in the group as if they were the purples, mauves, and grays in a paint box. He would slash across his canvas a great blue streak from the driving clarinet of Bigard, followed by the dark brown tones of Tricky Sam's plunger, backed up, perhaps, by the liquid gold of Hodges's alto saxophone.

In his composing Duke was always very conscious of the colorful play of sound. For example, in the first theme of "The Mooch," recorded in 1928, about a year after the band went into the Cotton Club, a sinuous winding cry by the clarinet and saxophones is answered by Bubber Miley growling like a demented tiger into the plunger mute.

This theme is followed by a rather light solo by Ellington at the piano, which provides an extreme contrast with what has gone before. Then Barney Bigard plays a solo in the clarinet's low register, getting a smokey sound. Bubber comes on next, growling away, while Johnny Hodges plays answers to his phrases on the saxophone—the harsh trumpet wailing contrasting dramatically with the creamy flow of Hodges' saxophone. Finally, the piece returns to the first theme to wind things up.

"The Mooch" is a masterful demonstration of Ellington's ability to play with sound. Indeed, the piece is built on sound more than anything else. The melodies are really quite simple, and while the solos by Miley, Hodges, and the others are excellent, they would not of themselves be remarkable. What makes "The Mooch" a jazz classic is the way Duke has mixed his colors: The whole becomes greater than the sum of its parts.

A second skill Ellington showed right from the beginning was the daring and imaginative way he would blend various instruments in the orchestra. No composer in jazz, and few in any kind of music, has ever shown such skill in blending sounds. Dance band arrangers almost invariably "voiced" dance orchestras in sections. That is to say, first the trumpets would play a passage in harmony, then the saxophones would play, and so forth.

But Duke was always pulling one instrument out of a section and mixing it with instruments from other sections. The classic example of this is "Mood Indigo." (The tune was actually written by New Orleans clarinetist Lorenzo Tio, but it was Duke's arrangement of it that made it famous.)

The main theme of the tune could hardly be simpler, consisting of a very few notes played at a slow tempo. But Duke clothed the little melody with a fascinating sound, by combining muted trumpet, muted trombone, and clarinet. Such a voicing was unheard of in jazz at that point.

But Duke took it even a step further: Instead of giving the clarinet the lead in the middle or upper register, he let the muted trumpet take the lead, and had the clarinet play a harmony part in the low register. Why did he do this? It was because he realized that the sound of the clarinet in the low register was much closer to the smokey sound of the muted brass than it would be in the high register.

Duke put "Mood Indigo" together in the recording studio. The orchestra played it that night for the Cotton Club radio broadcast and it became an instant hit. And it was the way that Duke blended the instruments to produce a delicate, haunting sound that made the piece a success.

This playing with color, with new shades coming and going constantly, kept the music always shifting and changing. Ellington's music is never static, never sits still, but is always in motion. He added to this effect by contrasting themes, as well as colors. Most popular music of that time, and indeed today, is made up of two, or at most three, themes, usually in the same key, or with one modulation in and out of another key. Duke, on the other hand, very frequently switched keys dramatically, moving from a subdued or melancholy minor key, to a happier major key. He does this in "The Mooch," "East St. Louis Toodle-Oo," and many other pieces. And where key changes in most popular music are the obvious ones, from C to G, for example, Duke was always jumping into a distant key.

Probably his most famous piece of this sort from the early days is "Black and Tan Fantasy." It opens with a very funereal, dirgelike theme played by Miley in his growl style in a minor key. Then it jumps without preparation into a distant, quite surprising major key, which moves to yet another major key before the theme is finished. This theme is played by Toby Hardwick in his light, pretty manner. The two themes could hardly contrast more: one is melancholy, minor, harsh; the other is pretty, soft, and smooth. "Black and Tan Fantasy" was one of Duke's first hits and was singled out for special attention by the music critic Darrell and others, as demonstrating that jazz could be a true art.

One last thing that was important about Ellington's composing, was his skill at using his excellent soloists. He knew all their strengths and weaknesses. He knew that this one was strong in the upper register, this one adept at playing pretty melodies, but not so good at the hot ones. Indeed, he even claimed that he knew which notes a given musician was especially likely to get a good sound on. As he worked out his pieces in the studio, he would very carefully choose who ought to solo on which pieces, or on which themes in each piece. And if he was not getting exactly the quality he wanted, he would give the solo to another player. Most band leaders would simply call for a trumpet solo at a certain point; but Duke always knew which of his trumpeters he wanted to play at that place.

It can be seen, then, that Duke Ellington's compositional style was extremely personal. He was not, as most popular dance band arrangers did, working things out from theories, rules, systems; he was instead going by his own ideas, his own intuitions and feelings. He had always been a person with a lot of confidence in himself, and he was sure that if he liked a certain melody or sound, it was right. That was the key: If he liked it, that was the way it ought to be.

We must not, however, forget that the members of Duke's orchestra contributed a great deal to the mix. For example, Bubber Miley wrote the opening themes to both "East St. Louis Toodle-Oo," and "Black and Tan Fantasy." Toby Hardwick helped with "Sophisticated Lady." Several of the musicians, especially Harry Carney, contributed to "Rockin' in Rhythm," one of the band's most successful numbers.

Duke, however, was a proud man. Indeed, it is fair to say that he had a streak of vanity. He did not like to admit that he was dependent on others for anything, much less the ideas that went into his compositions. And unfortunately, at times this vanity led him to take credit for melodies that had initially been composed by others. Some of the members of the band came to resent the habit Ellington had of putting his name on things that were not, strictly speaking, his. But they so respected Duke that they rarely said anything about it publicly. And it must be borne in mind that in the end it was Ellington, and not anybody else who created the complete compositions that became jazz classics.

CHAPTER EIGHT

By the time Ellington opened at the Cotton Club he had brought his wife and his son, Mercer, to live with him in Harlem. But matters between him and his wife, Edna, were not good, and in 1929 they broke up. Duke took an apartment in the so-called Sugar Hill area, the most expensive place to live in Harlem, and his girlfriend, Mildred Dixon, moved in with him. However, he and Edna continued to be on fairly good terms, and Duke always saw to it that neither she nor Mercer lacked for money.

Then, in 1930, Duke brought his mother, father, and kid sister, Ruth, to live in New York with him. This move tells us much about Duke. Most young men do not bring their parents to live with them, unless they are aged or ill and need help. Duke's parents were in good health, and J.E. had an excellent job in Washington as a blueprint maker for the United States Navy. In fact, J.E. was reluctant to move. He knew he could not find as good a job in New York as his navy job, and he resisted coming to New York.

But Daisy Ellington doted on her son. Now he was becoming wealthy and celebrated, justifying her faith in him, and she was prouder of him than ever. She was eager to be with him in New York. Duke had always felt very close to her and wanted her nearby. Finally they persuaded J.E. to leave Washington, and they all moved in with Duke. J.E. was given a minor job helping with the band, and Duke was now, in a certain sense, the head of the family. He would always respect his father, but he controlled the money, not J.E. Just as Duke had managed to take over the Washingtonians and make it his band, so now he had taken charge of his own family. That was the way it would always be with Duke. He was proud, and he wanted always to be the ringmaster in command of the people around him. He was always very generous; he would see to it that "his" people, as he thought of them, would never be in want. For example, when he had to fire Sonny Greer from the band because he was drinking too much, he kept Sonny on the payroll and supported him for years. The same was true of other people who passed through his life and were in need. But he always had to be in charge. Both his son, Mercer, and his kid sister, Ruth, nineteen years younger than he, had to fight, as they grew, to escape from Duke's dominance.

But Duke, certainly, was also a hero in their eyes. He and the band were now attracting a great deal of attention. The group was chosen to accompany a musical comedy called *Liza,* written by the famous composer, George Gershwin. It made a short film called *Black and Tan Fantasy,* which was built around the famous tune. In 1930 the band traveled out to Hollywood to appear in a movie featuring a famous radio comic team, Amos 'n' Andy. The band was being written up in magazines and newspapers. In 1931 Duke was invited to visit President

Herbert Hoover in the White House as one of a group of "Negro leaders" in America. In 1932 his band was chosen by the readers of the *Pittsburgh Courier*, a newspaper for blacks, as the leading black band in the country, finally beating out the famous Fletcher Henderson Orchestra. In the same year a well-known classical composer named Percy Grainger arranged for Duke to play a concert at Columbia University and lecture on his music. Success was swarming in on him from every direction. When he had opened at the Cotton Club at the end of 1927, he had been known only to people in the New York music business, some of the jazz fans, and the gangland and show business people who had jammed the Kentucky Club night after night. When he left the Cotton Club in 1931 he was one of the most famous band leaders in America, whose music was loved by dancers and jazz fans, and written about respectfully by intellectuals and music critics.

It is important for us to understand why this was happening to Duke Ellington. As I pointed out earlier, there were other musicians in jazz who were thought by jazz fans to be as good as Duke or better. The Fletcher Henderson Orchestra had gotten there before Ellington, and always contained some brilliant soloists. Louis Armstrong, Bix Beiderbecke, Benny Goodman, King Oliver, and many others were considered more exciting improvisers than Duke. But it was Duke who was being asked to speak at universities, being invited to the White House.

In part, the answer lay in the fact that Duke Ellington was not just an improviser, but a composer, and composers were seen by many people as above simple improvisers. But at bottom, it was Ellington's personality—his pride, his self-confidence, his almost royal bearing, that made people take him more seriously than other jazz musicians. You could not look down on Duke; he simply would not permit it.

We can see the effects in his attitude toward the whole race question. Duke did occasionally have to face racial problems, especially during the Depression when the hard times of the 1930s made it necessary for the band to play one-nighters in the South. He could not, even though he had been invited to the White House, get into the best white hotels and restaurants even in the North, although that would soon begin to change.

But in the main, Ellington dealt with segregation by ignoring it. He had been raised to be proud of his black heritage, and again and again he celebrated his race in his music with such pieces as "Black Beauty," "The Harlem Suite," "Black, Brown, and Beige," and many more. But he was never a militant in the racial battle. He did not make speeches or statements about it, he did not march in demonstrations, he did not sign petitions. Duke's way of battling the color line was to rise above it. He told one interviewer, "You have to try not to think about [racial segregation] or you'll knock yourself out."

Once when the band was playing in Texas a big white man decided to make trouble. He walked over to the bandstand and snatched up Tricky Sam's trombone. "I'm gonna take this trombone with me," he told Duke. Duke replied, "Well, if that's the way you feel about it, there's the trombone. If you want it take it." The man handed the trombone back and the incident was over. But it was typical of the way Ellington handled racial problems—simply ignore them as much as possible.

The net result of all of this was that Duke Ellington had far greater acceptance in white society than most blacks did. He was not seen as an ordinary entertainer: he was seen instead as a composer, a sophisticated gentleman, an artist, somebody special or superior. By insisting on his own worth he conquered the racism around him, and in that way may have contributed more to the breaking down of walls than some more outspoken people.

Duke's way of presenting himself to audiences had another important effect on black entertainment. Going way back to the days of the minstrel shows, when blacks first began to establish themselves in show business, whites expected them to adhere to the image of the "humorous darky" as the term was then, who was scared of "h'ants," loved watermelon and fried chicken, and fought with razors. It was extremely difficult for black performers to depart from this stereotype. White audiences would not, as a rule accept a black as a performer of classical music, or an actor of Shakespearian tragedy. There were a few exceptions, like the famous Sissieretta Jones, who had a successful career singing concert music in the 19th century, and later on Paul Robeson, who was acting in serious dramatic roles at the time Ellington was at the Cotton Club. But these exceptions were rare: Most black performers worked more as clowns than serious performers. Such great black jazz musicians as Louis Armstrong and Fats Waller felt they had to do a lot of clowning around on the stage to amuse their audiences.

But this, assuredly, was not Duke Ellington's way. He would not mug, tell jokes, stomp around the stage. Instead, even when the music was at its hottest, he would present himself with that royal manner. On stage he at times dressed rather flamboyantly, as was the custom of dance bands at the time, but his usual garb was conservative suits and ties. He did not use a lot of slang, but spoke proper, indeed rather ornate, English. Duke was thoroughly aware of the old tradition of the watermelon-loving black performer, and he was absolutely determined to stay as far away from it as possible. The very fact that he was making such a success of himself without stooping to the stereotype encouraged other black performers to do the same. The old stereotype lingered, but by the time Ellington left the Cotton Club, it was beginning to die, in large part because of Duke's insistence on maintaining his dignity.

This sense of his own worth undoubtedly contributed to his desire to write something of what he considered a more serious type. If critics like Percy Grainger and R. D. Darrell thought his work was valuable, why shouldn't he try his hand at something outside of jazz? He did not know a great deal about classical music, but as always, he felt confident that he could bring something off if he tried. However, Duke was not the sort of man to drive himself hard, and in the end it was Irving Mills who provided the push. One day, not long after the Ellington band left the Cotton Club, Mills blandly announced that the band would shortly present a new, more classical work, "a rhapsody," according to Mills. His aim was not to drive Duke into writing symphonic works but to get some publicity for the band, which was no longer doing those radio shows from the Cotton Club.

Duke was now stuck, and he set about putting together a piece that was called "Creole Rhapsody." The piece was eventually issued on records in two fairly different versions. "Creole Rhapsody" got the attention that Mills and Duke hoped it would. It was seen by many critics as the first really successful attempt to merge jazz and classical music. The attempt had been made before: Indeed, for ten years Paul Whiteman had been claiming that his music was "symphonic jazz." But most serious jazz fans did not think that Whiteman's music had much jazz in it, except that provided by his soloists, like Bix Beiderbecke. "Creole Rhapsody" did contain a lot of good jazz, as well as the more symphonic elements, and the jazz people treated it respectfully. Not everyone of them agreed, but most did. And in the end, it won the New York Schools of Music's annual award for 1932 as the best new work by an American composer. It was final confirmation that Ellington was indeed somebody special.

Ellington's new fame was not confined to the United States. Across the Atlantic in England there was a small, but dedicated group of jazz fans who had by 1932 learned to appreciate hot music. And many of them saw Ellington as the leader in the field. They had been reading R. D. Darrell's reviews and articles about Ellington, they had gotten hold of his records and been amazed for themselves, and by 1932 some of his classics were being issued by English record companies. The English jazz critics in particular were excited by the possibilities they saw in "Creole Rhapsody." The English had not been hearing jazz in the way that Americans had for fifteen years; they were new to it, and it was easier for them to grasp in its more composed form, which suggested the classical music they were familiar with. It was the idea of many of them—as with many Americans, too—that "Creole Rhapsody," combining jazz and classical music, was the direction jazz ought to take.

Not surprisingly, as Mills began to read the glowing tributes Ellington was receiving in the English musicians' newspaper, *Melody Maker,* it occurred to him that the orchestra ought to make a tour of England. It would be profitable, would generate publicity, and would add to the band's prestige. So he worked out a deal with some British promoters, and a brief series of concerts was set up for the summer of 1933.

The musicians were elated by the idea of a trip abroad. They had heard that race prejudice did not exist in Europe, and they were eager to see for themselves. Duke himself was also pleased. At the time Europe had a certain stature in the eyes of many Americans, who assumed that Europeans were more cultivated than they were. After all, it was Europeans who had created so much of the culture Americans enjoyed—the plays of Shakespeare, the painting of Michelangelo, the symphonies of Beethoven. Ellington was excited by the challenge of playing his music for the English.

He was also nervous about the trip; Duke Ellington, for all of his good manners and sophisticated exterior, was a man of many superstitions. For example, he would not wear certain colors of clothing; he would not accept a gift of shoes, for that meant that the person might walk away from him; he was afraid of drafts and kept windows closed around him, even on hot days; he was afraid of flying in an airplane and would not do it until forced to by the long tours he made later in his career; and he was deathly afraid of being shipwrecked. But in those days, before transatlantic air flights, the only way to get to England was by ship. Duke spent most of the nights on the journey sitting up playing cards, in order to be awake if the ship started to go down.

But the ship did not sink. It arrived safely, and when the band got into London it was greeted by a mob of fans, photographers, and reporters. Unfortunately, very quickly the musicians discovered that England was not as free of racial prejudice as they had been told. No hotel could be found that would take in eighteen blacks (some of the Cotton Club dancers had been added to the show). Eventually Ellington was given a room in the prestigious Dorchester Hotel, but the other musicians were scattered around London in small hotels and rooming houses.

Nonetheless, while racial prejudice did exist in London—and in Europe in general—it was not so widespread nor held so strongly by many people as was the case in the United States. As a result the band, and especially Duke, was invited to parties and receptions given in their honor. The group played at Punch's Club, which was filled with members of the British aristocracy, and later went to a party attended by the Prince of Wales, who would soon be King Edward VIII of England. The

Prince of Wales liked jazz and played drums a little. He became friendly with members of the band, especially Duke and Sonny Greer, and sat in on Sonny's drums for awhile.

Duke and the others were thrilled by the attention they received from English nobility; but more important in the long run was the enthusiasm of a small group of English music critics who were avidly interested in jazz. These people spent a lot of time talking to Ellington and attended all of the concerts. They told him that they believed he was more than just a dance band arranger and composer. They insisted that his music was important and that he must take it seriously. One of them said that he was "the first real composer of uncommon merit, probably the first composer of real character to come out of America." Another one compared him to the famous modern composers of classic music, Stravinsky and Ravel.

The concerts in London were a great success. Fans leaving one of them tore at Ellington's clothes and leaped on his car as it drove away from the theater. The audiences were wildly enthusiastic about the music, and the houses were packed. From London the band went on to Holland and then Paris, where it played more concerts for enthusiastic audiences. Once again there were parties attended by celebrities, big write-ups in the newspapers and a lot of flattering attention from the small but eager groups of jazz fans in those countries. It was all very heady for the band; they had never experienced anything quite like it in the United States. And they left for home filled with good spirits.

But Ellington brought back with him more than high spirits. He returned to New York now convinced that he was not just the leader of a popular jazz band, but a real composer of serious music. He was determined to write more pieces like "Creole Rhapsody." Later on he said, "The main thing I got out of Europe was spirit. If they think I'm *that* important, then maybe

I have kinda been saying something, maybe our music does mean something." And he began thinking about new pieces in the symphonic mode.

It is important, however, to keep this European experience in perspective. For one thing, few of the European jazz fans and critics had ever visited the United States, and they had a lot of foolish ideas about the country: Ellington was hardly the "first real composer of uncommon merit" produced by America. For another thing, many of these European jazz enthusiasts did not understand the music as well as they thought they did, and they made a number of misjudgments about Duke's music that more knowledgeable Americans would not have made. Finally—and this was something Ellington himself did not realize—the interest in his music in Europe was confined to a very small group of people. In the United States he could fill theaters, dance halls, and nightclubs every night of the year; in Europe he could only attract large audiences for occasional concerts. The European promoters knew this, and they did not ask Ellington to come back for another six years.

Moreover, American critics like R. D. Darrell had been touting Ellington as a serious composer and comparing him to Ravel and Stravinsky for several years before the Europeans knew anything about him. Indeed, Darrell had wanted to write a book about Duke, but unfortunately Ellington did not respond to the idea. But somehow the enthusiasm of Americans for his music did not make a great impression on him. He was used to applause at home.

It was the praise of the Europeans that struck Duke. Like most Americans, he was impressed by the ladies and gentlemen of London and Paris, and their enthusiasm for his work mattered more than praise from Americans.

Paradoxically, the new spirit Ellington brought home from Europe did not immediately result in symphonic pieces on the order of "Creole Rhapsody." Instead, in a sudden creative flurry, he began to turn out a sequence of enduring jazz classics in the standard Ellington style.

One of these was "Rude Interlude," a play on the title of his early song, "Mood Indigo." Like the earlier piece, this is a very quiet, soft composition made of a minimum of musical material. It consists mainly of a two note figure repeated again and again in different guises—played higher or lower, passed around from one instrument to the next, clothed in shifting harmonies. Usually the brief figure is answered by another instrument, or group of instruments. Louis Bacon, a trumpeter who was not part of the orchestra, was brought into the studio to "scat" sing a wordless vocal in the manner of Louis Armstrong, to provide contrast. The piece is virtually motionless, drifting slowly along like a cloud coming into sight and going across the sky. The harmonies are very "close" and dissonant. By this time Duke was gaining mastery over chord structures and was growing very daring in the use of unusual harmonies.

Another masterpiece from this period was "Daybreak Express," a composition which demonstrates Ellington's extraordinary skill in dealing with pure sound. "Daybreak Express" is what is called program music—that is, it is supposed to sound like something beside pure music. In this case it is a railroad train. Duke may have been scared to fly and worried that ships might sink, but he loved to travel on trains. In those days the most popular bands, the ones who were making good incomes, traveled by special Pullman cars. Sometimes they had their own baggage cars to hold the instruments, music stands, and their suitcases; and they had their own provisions for meals.

This means of transportation was particularly important for black musicians, who might find it difficult getting rooms or going into good restaurants in many cities, especially in the

South. Closed off in their own Pullmans, they could eat, drink, play cards, chat, or sleep safe from the problems of segregation.

As the Duke Ellington band grew successful, Duke had his own private compartment on the train. Here he would sit alone night after night listening to the sounds the train made as it raced through the darkness. Barney Bigard said later:

> He would hear how the train clattered over the crossing and he'd get up and listen to the engine. He'd listen as it pulled out of the station huffing and puffing, and he'd start building from there.

"Daybreak Express" was built on those memories of nights on the train. As the piece opens we hear the train begin to slide out of the station, gathering speed. Cootie Williams growls a little train whistle, and the train starts to race along. In this part Ellington intermingles three separate voices—a high trumpet note, followed by the brass and then the saxes in the first chorus, and in the second chorus brass, saxes, and the trumpet high note. It is all quite complicated, but so sure was Duke's sense of sound that we can almost see that train speeding along through the countryside.

During the very creative period following the trip to England, Ellington wrote two of his best-known songs, "Solitude," and "In a Sentimental Mood." The melody to "Solitude" is very simple. Its main effect comes from the movement of the leading tone (Ti) rising up to the tonic (Do). But it is very deftly, if simply, harmonized and has always been one of Duke's most popular songs. "In a Sentimental Mood" is a pretty song and also has been quite popular. It is probable that Toby Hardwick contributed portions of the melody.

The Duke Ellington we are seeing in these pieces from 1933 had matured substantially as a composer from the beginner he was in the early days at the Cotton Club. He had by now spent thousands of hours working with his orchestra to compose his pieces, thousands of hours at the piano experimenting with harmony and melody, thousands of hours sitting on those trains late at night thinking about music and composing in his head. He had gone to a music conservatory in which the teacher was Ellington and the only pupil Duke. He had done it his own way, but by 1933 he had become a master of, if not music in general, at least the short three-minute jazz piece that was the basic stock in trade of his orchestra. It was all coming together, and over the next ten years Ellington would create a sequence of jazz masterpieces. But he had still not written the longer, symphonic pieces that the English critics were urging him to undertake.

CHAPTER NINE

Professionally Duke was skyrocketing to the top. But personally he was about to suffer a devastating loss. Not long after the band returned from England, it became clear that his beloved mother, Daisy Ellington, was ill. Through 1934 she grew increasingly worse. At first Daisy refused to go to a hospital, but by the fall of 1934 it was plain that something had to be done. She was examined and it was discovered that she had cancer.

Duke was in anguish. He sent her to a cancer research center in Detroit where she could get the most advanced treatment. In those days, however, much less was known about cancer than is known today, and cures were rare. By the beginning of 1935 it was clear that Daisy did not have much longer to live. Late in May Duke simply left the band and went out to Detroit. He spent three days in the hospital, never leaving his mother's side, and at moments sleeping with his head on the pillow next to hers. Finally she died.

For Duke it was a staggering blow. Daisy Ellington had been at the center of his life. She mattered to him more than any other person ever had, or ever would. She was the central star in his sky; and she had blinked out. For days he could not stop crying. He said, "I have no ambition left. When mother was alive I had something to fight for, I could say, 'I'll fight with anybody, against any kind of odds' . . . Now what? I can see nothing. The bottom's out of everything." It was clear that much of what he had achieved had been done to please his mother. And now he could no longer please her.

The effects are easy to see in his music. The sudden creative flurry which came after the English trip abruptly halted. From the time of his mother's death through the remainder of the year he cut only three sides, none of them important ones. He continued to lead the band out of habit, and because he had developed a lavish life-style which took a lot of money to keep up. But he was just going through the motions.

However, his mother's death finally inspired him to write a new symphonic piece in the manner of "Creole Rhapsody." Not long after Daisy died the band embarked on a tour of the South, traveling by Pullman car in the usual fashion. Duke, still filled with grief, sat in his compartment night after night thinking. "I found the mental isolation to reflect on the past," he said. "It was all caught up in the rhythm and motion of the train dashing through the South, and it gave me something to say that I could never have found words for."

He called the piece that came out of his memories of his mother, and his boyhood, "Reminiscing in Tempo." It was written in four sections, to be issued as four sides of the three-minute 78 rpm records of the time. And it illustrates both the strengths and weaknesses of Duke's attempts to write these longer, symphonic kinds of pieces.

"Reminiscing in Tempo" is built around two nicely contrasting themes, which keep coming and going, with some variation. It is not a very jazzy piece. There are not many improvised solos and much of it is played without the usual swing that the Ellington band produced. The harmonies are interesting, and advanced for music of this kind.

The problem with "Reminiscing in Tempo" is structure. Classical music does not depend upon melody and harmony alone. Crucial to the success of longer works, like symphonies, is what is called "form"—that is to say, the shape of the piece. A soundly constructed classical work is made up of smaller parts that relate to each other in some clear way. One common form for music to take is "theme and variation," in which a main theme is stated, and then is played again in several different ways—in a minor key, in a different meter, and so forth. Another way of giving a longer work form is to have the music circle away from the main theme, perhaps going through a number of keys, until it arrives back where it began. There are, obviously, lots of ways of giving a piece of music some kind of form. And composers frequently build their music around a series of rising and falling climaxes, working up to a big final one.

This sense that the music is following a pattern gives listeners the feeling that it is going somewhere and helps to hold their attention. In a good classic piece the parts cannot be shuffled around arbitrarily, any more than the words in a sentence can be shifted around on the toss of a card.

Duke Ellington never fully grasped this idea; or if he did, he proved not to be skilled enough to make it work in his longer pieces. This is not to say that he lacked talent; he had plenty of that. But learning how to construct a major piece of music takes a lot of concentrated study. It is not something that comes to anyone naturally. To learn it, it is necessary to analyze a great many masterworks, which is exactly what students at conservatories do.

Duke, as we have seen, would never put himself under the direction of anybody. Furthermore, he had not studied classical music at all—indeed, had never listened to very much of it. He could have learned what he needed to know, but he had neither the time nor the inclination to do so.

As a consequence, many critics have said that Duke's longer pieces lack that essential ingredient, form. Without a carefully worked out structure, these critics say (and I agree), such pieces cannot succeed, because they do not appear to be going anywhere.

Duke tried to give most of his symphonic pieces some kind of shape by giving them a "program." Many of them were supposed to represent a scene, a mood, an event. This is a perfectly acceptable idea—famous works like "The 1812 Overture" and Beethoven's Fifth Symphony are supposed to reflect events and themes. But a longer work cannot depend on its program to hold it together; it must work as a piece of music as well.

This is the problem with "Reminiscing in Tempo." It rambles; the parts do not seem to be there for any particular reason, except that they sound good. Of course a man with Ellington's talent was bound to write interesting melodies and clothe them in striking harmonies. Thus along the way through "Reminiscing in Tempo" there are many lovely passages; but it is hard to hear what binds them together. It is the difference between looking at a series of snapshots of nice views and seeing a travel movie that takes you from one place to the next.

Unhappily, both the critics and the jazz fans were perturbed by "Reminiscing in Tempo." In particular, the English critics, who had been instrumental in urging Ellington to write longer, symphonic works, were extremely critical of the piece. It was, needless to say, a great disappointment to Ellington, and it would be several years before he tried another work of this kind.

On top of his other troubles, Duke Ellington was now faced with new competition. A look back at the earlier history of jazz will show what happened.

The first jazz bands were little groups using one to three horns over a rhythm section and playing mainly improvised music. However, by the mid-1920s Americans were demanding for dancing and shows larger orchestras playing music arranged for seven to ten horns, and rhythm. By the end of the 1920s these bands, playing a lot of hot music, were the most popular ones, although the old small band jazz was still being played to some extent.

In 1929 the United States was struck by the economic cataclysm known as the Depression. Millions of Americans lost their jobs, and most of those who kept their jobs had their salaries sharply cut. Naturally, people had less money to spend for records and on going out to dance. Besides, a new medium had come along that supplied entertainment free: radio. People were listening to bands like Ellington's, from the Cotton Club and elsewhere, and dancing at home. Many nightclubs and dance halls closed, the record industry collapsed, and a lot of orchestras were forced to disband. The Ellington group was one of the few that flourished during the early days of the Depression. Indeed, in the first half of the 1930s Duke had the field of the hot dance band almost to himself.

But then, in 1935 clarinetist Benny Goodman had a huge, sudden success with a new orchestra playing a kind of music based on the big hot bands of the 1920s, but with a somewhat different kind of lilt, or "swing," to it. Goodman's music came to be called swing, and his orchestra a swing band. Very quickly other musicians formed their own swing bands in order to follow after Goodman's success. By the later years of the 1930s swing was America's popular music, washing everything else aside. There were at least fifty nationally known swing bands touring the country, and hundreds more working in their own areas and hoping to become national successes. The Duke Ellington Orchestra had been there ahead of the rest. Duke himself was a star, and his sidemen were celebrities to jazz fans. But the Ellington Orchestra was not truly a swing band: Duke's musical ideas were too original and individual for his band to fit into any mold. For example, the swing bands built a lot of their numbers, especially the hot pieces, out of "riffs"—short, repeated phrases that produced a driving rhythm. Duke used far fewer riffs in his work than the swing bands, and far more counterpoint—two or more melodies going along at once as in the opening section to "Daybreak Express." For another, Ellington had tailored his band around the unique styles of his musicians. Where a swing band arrangement might call for a trumpet solo, which could be played by any of the trumpeters in the orchestra, Ellington always knew exactly which trumpeter he wanted at a given point. This practice helped to give his orchestra a sound that could never be confused with another one. For a third thing, where the swing bands stuck mostly to rather simple harmonies, the ones dancers were used to, Ellington was very adventurous in finding new and quite dissonant harmonies, at least for popular music.

Thus, the Ellington band was not really playing swing music much of the time. Many of the young people who roared after Goodman and the others did not quite understand what Ellington was doing, and preferred to dance to bands whose music was a littler easier for them to grasp. It was not exactly that Duke lost popularity; he continued to have a large following. It was that the other bands caught up to him, and then passed him. By the end of the 1930s, leaders like Benny Goodman, Glenn Miller, and Tommy Dorsey were ahead of Ellington in the swing band race.

But Duke Ellington was not the sort of person who would

allow himself to imitate anyone. He would pick up ideas from here and there, but he would always reshape the idea and add to it, to make it his own. He continued to press forward in his own direction, and in the long run it would pay off.

There were, in the early days of the swing period, some changes to the orchestra. Unhappily, Arthur Whetsol, who had been one of the original Washingtonians, began to suffer from a brain tumor. He was forced to leave the band and very soon died. Freddy Jenkins also became ill, and had to leave, and although he eventually got his health back, he was not able to play trumpet any longer. Duke then brought in a trumpeter named Rex Stewart, who had worked with a number of top bands, including Fletcher Henderson's. Stewart was a typical Ellington choice—a strong player with a dramatically individual sound. Stewart not only worked with a variety of mutes, but had developed a system of playing in which he pushed the trumpet valves only partway down. This was known as "half-valving," and gave the trumpet a peculiar sound. Stewart did not invent half-valving. It had been done by many trumpeters before, among them Louis Armstrong, whom Stewart vastly admired. But other trumpeters usually employed the half-valve device only occasionally, to add a bit of spice to a melody. Stewart, on the other hand, would at times play a whole melody with the half valves. He does this on his most famous solo, which he worked out with Duke, called "Boy Meets Horn."

Another important addition to the band at this moment was trombonist Lawrence Brown. People commonly have the idea that jazz musicians are likely to be carefree and irresponsible, prone to drinking and using drugs. And it is certainly true that some jazz musicians hurt their careers and themselves by abusing drugs and alcohol. We have seen how liquor drastically shortened the career of Bubber Miley.

But playing a musical instrument as well as the people in the top bands had to require a lot of discipline, and indulgence in drink and drugs does not help. Lawrence Brown was an example of a musician who was raised to have the necessary discipline. His father was a preacher, and he grew up in a strict religious household. He never drank or smoked, but instead worked hard at his music. His father, unfortunately, disliked jazz, which he considered "the Devil's music," as did many religious people at that time. When Lawrence first became interested in popular music he would sneak out of his bedroom at night and slip off to a dance hall or theater to hear his favorite bands. Eventually his father found out what he was doing, and told Lawrence he must either give up playing dance music or leave home. Leaving home would be hard; but Brown was too deeply in love with jazz to give it up, and he left.

His hard work paid off. He developed a smooth, rich legato style—that is to say he did not attack his notes sharply, but let them flow from one into the next. This style contrasted markedly with the plunger mute antics of Tricky Sam Nanton, and the light, rather polite playing of Juan Tizol, and gave Duke yet another tone color to work with.

Another addition to the band at this time was tenor saxophonist Ben Webster. In the early days of jazz the trumpet, or cornet, was seen as the leading instrument; jazz "kings" were usually cornet players. But during the 1920s saxophones became increasingly popular, and by the 1930s the tenor saxophone was becoming the essential jazz instrument. Duke had never really had a true tenor saxophonist; clarinetist Barney Bigard could play the instrument capably when necessary, but he always preferred to play his solos on the clarinet.

Ben Webster had played with a number of important bands, but he had long wanted to play with the great Ellington Orchestra. He kept asking Duke for a job, but Ben was working for Cab Calloway, whom Duke was friendly with, and Duke didn't want to take a musician from a fellow band leader. He told Webster, "If you're ever out of a job, come and see me." In time Webster left the Calloway orchestra, because he was not getting as much chance to play solos as he wanted, and very quickly Duke hired him.

Ben Webster was an entirely different sort of person from the other recent arrival, Lawrence Brown. He was a heavy drinker and sometimes when he was drunk he'd lose his temper and start a fight. Many other musicians were afraid of him, because he seemed so tough, and they nicknamed him "the Brute." But he could also be kindhearted and gentle.

He played with a style that reflected both sides of his personality. On ballads he played with warm, soft breathy sound, but on fast tunes he sometimes used a harsher sound and drove very hard. Once again Ellington had found a musician who gave him a new tone color to work with, for Webster's sound contrasted markedly with the smooth, sinuous sound of Johnny Hodges, or the light touch of Toby Hardwick.

At about this time Duke changed bassists, bringing in a young man named Jimmy Blanton, who some of the bandsmen had discovered playing in a small nightclub in St. Louis. Blanton would be with Duke for only a few years, for he died young, but in that brief period he changed jazz bass playing. At that time many bass players had started on the tuba. They tended to think in terms of quarter notes plunked down on each beat, or on every other beat.

Blanton, however, had begun as a violinist, and he approached the bass as if it were a violin. Instead of playing one note per beat, he picked out more complex melody ideas, some of which involved playing at what seemed at the time to be very fast tempos. It was all very startling to other bass players. Duke wrote several pieces to feature Blanton, such as "Pitter

Panther Patter," and "Jack the Bear." The modern style of jazz bass playing developed out of the work of Jimmy Blanton. The new people coming into the band in the late 1930s were not merely fine players: They were among the best on their instruments of that time. As great as the Ellington band had been before, it was now even better. By 1940 Duke had the finest group of jazz musicians ever to be assembled into one ongoing band. He had some challengers. The Count Basie band of the same period had such great soloists as Lester Young and Buck Clayton, and what many jazz critics consider to be the best rhythm section of the swing era. The Benny Goodman orchestra of the early 1940s had some superb players, including Charlie Christian, who first demonstrated what could be done with the electric guitar, Duke's own Cootie Williams, and of course Goodman himself. The various Fletcher Henderson orchestras of the late 1920s and early 1930s had some of the finest jazz musicians of the period. And the "Herds" of Woody Herman of the 1940s had a number of wonderful jazz musicians, like saxophonist Stan Getz and trombonist Bill Harris.

But this Ellington band had three Hall of Famers in Johnny Hodges, Cootie Williams, and Jimmy Blanton. Barney Bigard, Rex Stewart, Lawrence Brown, and others were not far behind. There was Tricky Sam Nanton, one of the great masters of the plunger mute. And we must not forget the ringmaster of this great circus, Duke himself.

Coming into this impressive stable about this time was one other figure who would be important to Ellington. That was Billy Strayhorn, a young composer. Strayhorn had studied music while in high school in Pittsburgh. He had written some songs for a high school show. Once when Duke was playing a theater in Pittsburgh a friend urged Strayhorn to go backstage and show Duke his work. Billy felt shy about it but was persuaded to try. He played for Duke his now-famous song, "Lush Life." Ellington was impressed and told Billy to come see him if he ever got to New York. Billy spent the next year studying arranging, and then he found the courage to go to New York to see Duke Ellington. Duke hired him immediately. Very quickly Strays, as the bandsmen sometimes called him, became indispensable to Duke. Not only did he write some classic songs for Duke, like "Take the A Train," which became Ellington's theme, but he helped Duke in many other ways, writing arrangements for the band or collaborating with Duke on the symphonic pieces. A great deal of music which was issued under Duke's name was actually written by Billy Strayhorn. It is difficult to know exactly what he wrote, however, because he and Duke worked very closely. Once Duke called Billy from out of town and asked him to work up a theme for one of his sacred pieces, to the words "In the Beginning God . . ." The melody that Billy wrote was very close to the one Duke himself was working out, even though they had never discussed it.

Billy Strayhorn never cared who got credit for the work. He admired Ellington so much that he was happy just to be able to work with him.

By 1940 Duke Ellington had what many jazz critics today consider the finest large jazz orchestra ever to exist. Over the next few years Duke would create with this marvelous music machine some of the greatest jazz classics of all time, which would put him back on the top of the heap.

CHAPTER TEN

In the years around 1940 Duke Ellington reached his maturity as an artist. Many jazz musicians create their best work when they are quite young— in their early twenties or even in their late teens.

But Ellington's main work was not playing improvised jazz solos, but the much more complicated business of organizing fourteen or more musicians to produce music. It is an art that takes longer to learn. But by 1940 Duke had been leader of his own band without a break for fifteen years. He had written scores of pieces for his orchestra, dozens of popular songs, some of which had become big hits, as well as such extended or symphonic works as "Creole Rhapsody" and "Reminiscing in Tempo." He had been immersed in music day after day for years, and he had completely mastered the art of composing for the large jazz orchestra. It is therefore not surprising that in the period from the late 1930s to the early 1940s the band produced one masterpiece after another—hot swingers like "Main Stem," "Cotton Tail," and Perdido"; hard-driving blues such as "Things Ain't What They Used To Be," complex mood pieces like "Chelsea Bridge" and "Warm Valley," and fine popular tunes like "Don't Get Around Much Anymore," and "I Let a Song Go Out of My Heart." So much good music came out of this band that it is impossible to discuss it all, but we can look at some of it.

One of the most interesting of these pieces is one Duke called "Harlem Airshaft." Ellington, not surprisingly for a painter, liked making musical pictures of things—we remember "Daybreak Express," his famous tone portrait of a train. "Harlem Airshaft" is another musical picture. An air shaft in a big city apartment is simply an enclosed space running up between two adjoining buildings from ground floor to the roof, with the sky visible above. The idea is to let sunlight and air penetrate to all the rooms of each apartment. Especially in summer, when everybody's windows are open on the air shaft, all kinds of sounds, sights, and smells would echo up and down the air shaft.

Duke liked to observe what was going on in the air shaft. He said:

> So much goes on in a Harlem air shaft. You get the full essence of Harlem in an air shaft. You hear fights, you smell dinner. . . . You hear intimate gossip floating down. . . . You see your neighbors' laundry. . . . You smell coffee. . . . You hear people praying, fighting, snoring. Jitterbugs are jumping up and down. . .

Duke has very cleverly put this effect of variety and confusion into this piece. Notice how the music keeps jumping around from one instrument to the next. Themes appear suddenly and disappear as suddenly. There are surprising "breaks," when the music stops altogether for an instant. A good example of this is in the chorus where the trombones play the main melody while clarinetist Bigard swirls around them, and the saxophones chatter underneath.

Duke Ellington had a knack of making something very magical out of quite simple material. "Harlem Airshaft" is based on the blues chords, with a very simple bridge added. But by the time Duke gets finished piling up the sounds, it becomes a vital and interesting piece of music.

The same is true of one of Duke's most celebrated masterpieces, "Cotton Tail." The piece is based on a famous tune by George Gershwin, "I've Got Rhythm," which jazz musicians have always liked improvising on. Duke turns it into something more than a good popular tune. The piece starts abruptly, without any introduction of any kind, a very unusual thing to occur in this kind of music. Once again we see Duke breaking rules. The melody that opens the piece is much more interesting than the tune Gershwin wrote. The Gershwin melody goes up the scale a few notes and comes back down again; Ellington's melody keeps changing direction. Next Cootie Williams plays one of his famous growl solos. We expect this to be followed by a repeat of the opening melody, but suddenly Duke gives us a brand-new theme. This in turn is followed by one of the most famous tenor saxophone solos in jazz, by Ben Webster. But the high point is yet to come—a long, sinuous chorus for the saxophones which keeps twisting and turning like a snake looking for a way out of a maze. Once again Duke has created a varied, novel, and exciting piece of jazz on a very simple structure.

A record considered by many of Ellington's fans to be one of the greatest of all of his works is "Ko-Ko." It has never been clear what the title meant. However, Duke originally intended this work to be part of a musical history of black people, and he probably thought the term had some African significance. Like "Cotton Tail" and "Harlem Airshaft," it is built on a very simple foundation, in this case a blues in a minor key. But by the time Duke finishes with it, it has become a very complex piece of music.

There are two things to notice about the piece. The first of these is that in most of the choruses one or more instruments is holding a note most of the time. As the choruses come along the note being held is increasingly dissonant—that is to say, farther and farther away from the basic blues harmony.

The second point about this work is that it is built up by "layering"—in which groups of instruments keep piling new ideas and phrases one on top of another. But we are always able to hear these layers separately, shifting back and forth across each other. The music is constantly in motion, and because it is so dissonant it may be difficult for the inexperienced ear to grasp. But it is a wonderful piece of music, going far beyond the much simpler stuff being turned out by ordinary dance orchestras.

The Duke Ellington Orchestra had, in the early years of the 1940s, reached a peak. Through these years the band was repeatedly named as the best in America by the readers of *Down Beat* magazine, and the great soloists in the band, like Johnny Hodges and Barney Bigard, were often voted the top players on their instruments. In 1939 a biography of Duke was published. *Down Beat* carried a story on the band in almost every issue, many of them on its front page. The band was always in demand for movies, and in 1940 it grossed a million dollars, a huge sum at a time when an ice-cream cone cost a nickel, and a newspaper three cents. Duke was at the top.

He was, furthermore, increasingly being written about as an *artist*. This is a hard term to define, but people meant by it that

Ellington was something more than the leader of a popular dance orchestra. This certainly was the case. Although Ellington had to write a lot of ordinary popular music to satisfy the people who came out to dance to it, many of his works, like "Harlem Airshaft" and "Ko-Ko" were deeper and more complex than the hit tunes other dance bands were playing.

Duke Ellington, as we have seen, always insisted on being respected. He carried himself royally and insisted on traveling first-class. Similarly, he liked thinking of himself as a composer of serious music rather than as just a dance band leader. But in order to prove it, he would have to write more serious kinds of pieces.

For some time he had been thinking vaguely about composing a long piece that would describe the history of American blacks, or *Negroes,* to use the term Ellington preferred. "Ko-Ko" was originally written as part of this planned history of the American Negro.

But as ever, Duke was slow about getting much more of it written. He loved music; he loved working with the band, but he also liked good times—going out to restaurants, sitting around with his friends, talking, playing cards. He once admitted, "I can't get anything done unless I have a deadline." So time went by, with Duke getting very little done on his new long piece.

But many people were convinced that he had the talent to become a major composer of serious American music. They kept urging him to keep at his piece. Finally, in the fall of 1942 Duke agreed to buckle down to work. His agent arranged for it to be performed in Carnegie Hall in New York City in January of the next year. Carnegie was the most famous concert hall in the United States, home of the New York Philharmonic. Although a few jazz concerts had been given there before, the idea of a jazz musician performing a piece of serious music there was unusual. The proposed Ellington concert stirred up a great deal of interest, not only among jazz fans, but among symphony lovers as well.

Ellington now had only a few months in which to complete the work. Frantically he wrote and rehearsed it wherever and whenever he could—backstage in theaters between shows, late at night after the band finished playing a dance. Sometimes he even rehearsed parts of it during a dance, presenting the section as just another new dance piece; nobody was ever the wiser.

He was working in his usual way—not sitting down and writing out every note that was to be played, but working it out at the piano, and sketching out enough of it so he could feed it to the musicians at rehearsal. This meant that the piece would have to be played by his own orchestra, as there would be no complete score to present to another group. But it would make for an original and highly individualistic piece.

He worked on it right up until the last minute, still writing the final bits and pieces on the day of the concert. It was called "Black, Brown, and Beige" and was described by Ellington as "a tone parallel to the history of the American Negro." The first movement, called "Black," was meant to represent the early history of blacks in the United States, and contained portions reflecting church spirituals. The second section, "Brown," was meant to portray the contributions of blacks to various American wars. The "Beige" section described the modern life of blacks, including their spiritual yearnings and their desire for education.

The concert got a great deal of publicity, and the hall was filled with celebrities, including Eleanor Roosevelt, the president's wife, and the famous conductor Leopold Stokowski. It was a great moment for Duke Ellington. Twenty years earlier he had been an apprentice pianist working in an obscure band in a Harlem nightclub; now he was performing his own work before a crowd of celebrities in one of the most famous concert halls in the world.

But unhappily, the critics did not like "Black, Brown, and Beige." The jazz writers were loyal and said good things about it, but the symphonic critics disliked it. It was the old story: There was lots of wonderful music in "Black, Brown, and Beige," but as a whole it didn't hang together.

The arrows of the critics hurt; but Duke Ellington was a proud man and would not let anyone see the wounds. Instead, he went on tinkering with "Black, Brown, and Beige," trying to improve it. When he finally got around to recording it he used only certain portions of it—the more carefully composed parts that could stand up as songs on their own.

Probably the best of these was the section called "Come Sunday," which reflected the mood of quietness of a Sunday morning when people were on the way to church. "Come Sunday" was played by Johnny Hodges on alto saxophone. Hodges, by this time, was one of the most superb saxophonists that jazz has ever produced. He was able to create a smooth, sinuous sound that poured in a stream from the horn, and his playing of Duke's enchanting melody made it the high point of the concert. Duke would go on playing "Come Sunday" for the rest of his life.

There were other fine parts to "Black, Brown, and Beige"—a very pretty theme called "Sugar Hill Penthouse," some wonderful plunger playing by Tricky Sam Nanton on a work song, and a piece with a Latin beat called "The West Indian Influence." These pieces, too, Duke continued to play throughout his career.

Duke Ellington was not only a proud man, but a stubborn one. Whatever the critics thought, he was determined to go on producing these longer, symphonic works. For the next few years he brought a new piece to Carnegie Hall annually. After that these works came more sporadically, but they continued to come—he was revising one of his three "Sacred Concerts" as he lay dying. Perhaps the best known of these longer pieces were the three "Sacred Concerts" composed toward the end of his life; "Such Sweet Thunder" (also known as "The Shakespearian Suite"), which was supposed to depict various characters from Shakespeare's plays; "Suite Thursday," based on a novel called *Sweet Thursday;* and the "Far East Suite," meant to portray impressions gained during several tours of Asia, which many critics consider to be the best of these long works.

Today some critics and students of Ellington's music are beginning to insist that these extended works were underrated by critics of the time, and that many of them are excellent. Recordings of some of them are still available, and from time to time orchestras are put together to give concerts of one or another of them. It remains for the future to make a final judgment on these works.

CHAPTER ELEVEN

The interesting thing about "Black, Brown, and Beige," and the extended pieces that came along year after year, was that even though the critics did not like them, they enhanced Ellington's reputation as a serious composer. People were beginning to speak of him in the way that they talked about symphonic masters like Igor Stravinsky and Claude Debussy. Even Ellington's most ardent fans would not, probably, have claimed that "Black, Brown, and Beige" was in a class with Stravinsky's "Rites of Spring" or Debussy's "Sunken Cathedral"; but many were now insisting that Ellington should be given the same serious consideration that the others got.

In the early 1940s, Duke was on top of the mountain. Jazz critics, musicians, and fans were saying that his band was the greatest one in the history of jazz, and that records like "Harlem Airshaft" and "Ko-Ko" were jazz masterpieces. Many people who were interested in classical music were saying that he was one of the best American composers of his time. And the general public was clamoring for his records, mobbing dance halls to dance to his music, and crowding theaters to see the great band in action.

But just as Duke's career was rising to the top, troubles began to crowd in. For one thing, the United States had been drawn into World War II in December 1941. By the next year musicians were being drafted into the armed forces, the army was soaking up the gas, tires, and railroad cars that were essential to traveling bands; dancers sometimes did not have enough gas to drive twenty or thirty miles to their favorite dance halls or nightclubs.

For a second thing, because of a conflict between the musicians' union and the record companies, the recording industry ground to a halt. Duke could not record his band, and as a consequence it made no records for two years, although later home recordings made from radio broadcasts were discovered and issued.

But the most important problem facing Duke at this time was the departure of most of the great musicians who had been so important to the band. Cootie Williams got an offer from Benny Goodman at a much higher salary and left. Barney Bigard got married and wanted to come off the road to spend time with his wife. Johnny Hodges now had a big enough name to establish a band of his own. Duke and the belligerent Ben Webster quarreled frequently, and in time Duke felt he had to fire Ben, although he was sad at having to lose the great tenor man. Tricky Sam Nanton died. And eventually Juan Tizol and the irrepressible Toby Hardwick, who had worked with Duke since the old days in Washington thirty years before, also quit.

Duke had no trouble finding replacements for these men. Jimmy Hamilton, a fine, smooth-toned clarinet player, took over Bigard's spot, and stayed with Duke for twenty-five years.

To fill Cootie's shoes Duke found trumpeter Ray Nance, an all-around showman who sang, danced, and also played violin. Claude Jones replaced Tizol, and several trombonists attempted to capture Tricky Sam's plunger sound; Quentin Jackson came closest.

But no band could lose Johnny Hodges, Cootie Williams, Ben Webster, Tricky Sam Nanton, and Barney Bigard and remain the same. Part of the problem was this: In the beginning Duke had always reached out for musicians with strongly individual styles and built his pieces around those styles. Now, if he wanted to play a piece like "Don't Get Around Much Anymore," which had featured Hodges, he had to get somebody to imitate Hodges; if he wanted to play "Ko-Ko," he had to find a trombonist who could copy Nanton's plunger sound. And in few cases were the imitators able to play these solos as well as the original men could.

Duke's new pieces could be built around the new players; and in time some of the old hands came back, among them Hodges and Cootie Williams. But by the late 1940s musicians were coming and going so fast that jazz fans could hardly keep up with the changes. The band was in turmoil, and critics were beginning to say that Duke Ellington's music sounded tired and stale. In 1949 *Down Beat* said bluntly, "Isn't it about time the Ellington orchestra was disbanded before what's left of a great reputation is completely dragged in the muck?"

Making the problem worse was the fact that the swing band movement came to an abrupt end in 1946. Part of the problem was that a new type of jazz, called bebop, had suddenly appeared around 1945. The younger jazz fans took it up, and bebop has remained at the heart of jazz ever since. Duke and the swing band leaders seemed to many jazz fans and musicians to be old hat, playing a music that had had its day.

But the main difficulty was that times were changing. A

new generation of pop music fans was not interested in the swing bands, which they saw as belonging to their parents' generation. What they wanted were dreamy ballads sung by good-looking young men and women, such as Vic Damone, Perry Como, Patti Page, Jo Stafford, and others. Through 1945 and 1946 the swing bands collapsed one after another, until by the end of the 1940s there were only three of the well-known ones left: the Stan Kenton and Woody Herman orchestras playing a modern kind of swing which reflected the new bebop; and the Duke Ellington Orchestra. In time both the Kenton and Herman bands would also fail, although Herman, for the rest of his life, would revive his band from time to time.

But the Ellington band survived. Like the other big bands it was, by the end of the 1940s, losing money. But unlike the others, it had a leader who had an outside income. By this time Duke had written a long list of "standards," tunes that were not just quick hits, but continued to be played year after year. Among these were "Mood Indigo," "Solitude," "Sophisticated Lady," "Don't Get Around Much Anymore," and "I'm Beginning to See the Light." The income from these songs was large, and it enabled Duke to keep the band going.

This tells us something about Duke. Most other leaders in his situation would have given up the band and retired to live off income from the songs. But Duke was never really interested in money as such. He liked to live well: to buy the finest clothes, to stay at the best hotels, to eat at the best restaurants. But he never cared to pile up money in a bank account. The most important thing for Duke was to have his band so he could go on composing and playing his own music. It was the music that mattered, and so he poured the income from his songs into the band. As a result, the Ellington orchestra was the only one from the swing era which never broke up. It lasted continuously from the moment it opened at Barron's Exclusive Club as the Washingtonians in 1923 until Duke's final illness in 1974, a record no other American band has ever matched. But keeping the band together became increasingly difficult. By the early 1950s another type of music had come along to threaten the popularity of Duke's music. That was the rock and roll of Bill Haley and the Comets, Elvis Presley, and many others. By the 1960s the new rock music, starring the Beatles, would sweep away everything else so far as young people were concerned. Duke's record sales dropped. Hoping to improve the situation he began restlessly changing record companies. Morale in the band went downhill. Many of the musicians did not see themselves as stars in a great jazz band anymore. They came and went. Critics complained; audiences grew smaller; recording sessions came farther apart. The band was still working, for there were plenty of the old fans around who wanted to hear the old favorites—"Mood Indigo," "Rockin' In Rhythm," "Don't Get Around Much Anymore." But the band was not attracting the young people.

Then something happened. In 1954 a young jazz fan named George Wein got the idea of putting on a jazz "festival." The idea of music festivals was not new, for there had for some time been festivals of classical music put on at places like Tanglewood, Massachusetts, and Robin Hood Dell, near Philadelphia. But applying the idea to jazz was new.

Wein arranged for some wealthy people he knew to back the festival with money. These people had a large mansion in Newport, Rhode Island, where many very rich people had summer homes. It was decided that the festival would be held in Newport, and in that way the famous Newport Jazz Festival got started. (It is now held in New York City and other places under a different name.)

The Newport Jazz Festival got a lot of publicity and was a big success from the start. In 1956 the Ellington orchestra was invited to Newport to perform. Duke was to open the final Saturday night concert, then give way to other performers until the end of the evening, when he would again take the stage.

The groups which came in between the two Ellington stints played mainly an advanced, rather cool and intellectual kind of music. The audience was respectful but not terribly excited by this music. As it happened, these performances ran on longer than they should have. Duke, sitting idly by waiting for his turn at the end, was growing annoyed. The concert was supposed to be over at midnight, but the Ellington band did not even come on until quarter to twelve. Already people were beginning to leave.

Duke opened his performance with a piece called "The Newport Jazz Festival Suite," which he had worked out for the occasion. Then he called for another longer piece, called "Diminuendo and Crescendo in Blue," which was divided into two parts. Duke decided that in between the two parts his tenor saxophonist of the time, Paul Gonsalves, would play an up-tempo blues with just the rhythm section.

The band went into the first part of the number. The audience was enthusiastic but not uproarious. When this part was finished Ellington played a chorus of the blues to give Gonsalves time to get out of his chair and come down front. Then Gonsalves began to play a blazing hot solo with Duke and the rhythm section driving him forward. The audience began to get excited. Gonsalves wailed on. By the sixth chorus people were beginning to shout and clap their hands on the beat. Duke let Gonsalves blow on. People began to get up out of their seats and dance. Excitement mounted and kept on building. Gonsalves played a tenth chorus, a fifteenth chorus. By now scores of people were dancing in the aisles, and the rest were standing on their chairs to get a better view. Photographers were rushing around taking pictures and reporters were frantically scribbling in their notebooks. On Gonsalves rolled through the twentieth chorus, the twenty-fifth. The audience was shouting, waving their arms, clapping. It was a continuous roar.

Finally, after the twenty-seventh chorus Duke called for an end, and the band dived into the second part of "Diminuendo and Crescendo in Blue." At this point promoter Wein, fearful that the audience might actually riot—they were so worked up—asked Duke to stop. But the orchestra was rolling now and Duke kept the music coming. It was ninety minutes before the band left the stand. The audience was limp. As they finally began to leave, many of them were agreeing that it was the greatest jazz performance they had ever witnessed.

The key to it had been the six minutes of blues that Gonsalves had performed with the rhythm section—those blazing hot twenty-seven choruses. It says a great deal about jazz that after all the rather solemn, somewhat intellectual music that had gone before, it was this, the simplest kind of jazz played with drive and passion, that made the event one of the most memorable moments in jazz.

By the next day word was circulating that Duke Ellington was back. Newspapers wrote excited accounts of the Newport concert. *Down Beat* carried a big story on the event. Within weeks Duke was on the cover of *Time* magazine. After a long, dispiriting ten years, Duke Ellington was once again at the top of the heap.

Helping to improve things was the return of some of the old masters. Johnny Hodges's band did not prove to be successful, and he came back in 1955. Cootie Williams, after playing with Benny Goodman for a year, started a band of his own; this, too, proved a failure, and eventually he returned to Duke. Trombonists Juan Tizol and Lawrence Brown also came back. With some of the old voices in place, Duke was now able to recreate the famous pieces as they should be played.

Another improvement was the addition of drummer Sam Woodyard. He was not a subtle drummer, nor did he have the great technical skills of other drummers in jazz at the time. But he was a hard driver, and he gave the band a lift and a push that it had lacked for some time.

The band that Duke had in the late 1950s and into the 1960s was an improvement over the ones he had led in the previous ten years. It did not come up to the heights of the great bands of the 1930s and early 1940s—no band could have. But it was nonetheless a fine band. It included at various times such excellent jazz players as Cat Anderson, a trumpet high note specialist; Clark Terry, another trumpeter who also played the flügelhorn; and saxophonist Russell Procope, who filled in for Hodges in his absence. These later Ellington bands cut some memorable records, for example, "Lonesome Lullaby," one of those slightly melancholy, drifting pieces, like "Rude Interlude"; "Transblucency," which was supposed to suggest "a blue fog you can almost see through," and included a duet between Jimmy Hamilton's clarinet and Kay Davis's wordless vocal; and "Upper Manhattan Medical Group," featuring trumpeter Willie Cook. (The music fits the title.) During this period Duke also wrote some film music, including the scores to *The Anatomy of Murder* and *Paris Blues,* both of which got a good deal of publicity.

Still, there were problems. The 1950s had been a very good time for jazz, with many musicians doing extremely well playing jazz concerts, especially on college campuses. But in the 1960s the huge popularity of rock overpowered everything. Elvis Presley, then the Beatles, and then a whole series of groups like the Grateful Dead, the Doors, the Jefferson Airplane, the Rolling Stones, became hugely popular. Jazz lost its young audience, which it had always depended upon for support. To teenagers of the 1960s the Duke Ellington Orchestra was something from out of the distant past. And in truth, it must be admitted that many of the members of the band, including Duke himself, were old enough to be grandparents of the high school and college students of the time. Duke's following had by no means disappeared; it is simply that it had thinned out. Now he found it necessary to reach farther afield, and he began making regular visits to foreign countries. From the 1960s on almost every year he made long tours of Japan, Latin America, East Europe, Russia, and places he had always visited, like England and France. On many of these tours he was treated as an unofficial ambassador from the United States. He would be taken to meet princes, shahs, premiers; he would be given receptions and dinners by the American consuls in the cities he visited; he would be praised in speeches, would listen to special concerts of ethnic music by local musicians; he would be fussed over everywhere he went. He was now, by the 1960s, an international celebrity, a person whose name was known not just by jazz fans, but by all sorts of ordinary people who might not even know much about his music.

The same was true at home. By the 1960s the honors were rolling in on him so thick he could hardly keep track of them. He was given honorary degrees from more than fifteen colleges and universities. He was given the keys to eighteen cities, awards from seven states. He won uncounted fan and critic polls from *Down Beat, Playboy, Esquire,* and other magazines and groups. He was given a special blessing by the Pope, the President's Medal for Special Merit from Dwight D. Eisenhower, the President's Gold Medal from Lyndon B. Johnson, the Presidential Medal of Freedom from Richard M. Nixon. Indeed, President Nixon gave him a party at the White House in celebration of Duke's seventieth birthday. By then Duke Ellington had become one of the most famous musicians in the world.

CHAPTER TWELVE

By the 1960s Duke Ellington had concluded that his most important work was the extended, or symphonic, pieces he had been writing since "Creole Rhapsody" in 1931. It was getting to be an extensive body of work; it would eventually be enough to fill up about thirty records, quite a lot of music of this kind. To write and play this music he needed an orchestra, and to help support itself the orchestra had to continue to play dances, parties, nightclubs, and theaters as it had always done. This in turn meant spending more money, in order to transport it around the country. Duke was now carrying fifteen or more musicians, a barber, a band manager, a band boy to help carry the instruments, a lyricist to put words to his music, a friend or two, and others. It was like moving a small circus from place to place, and it was costing Ellington around a million dollars a year to keep this extensive organization going. But for Duke the critical thing was to have the band there to record his extended pieces, and he went on pouring the profits from his songs into the business.

By this time Duke had become more adept at writing out complete scores while sitting at the piano than he had been in the old days at the Cotton Club. He would more frequently bring to rehearsal chunks of music completely written out. But his basic method had not changed. He still wanted to hear how the music sounded, and he would constantly make changes, rewriting parts, or switching them around from section to section to hear how they sounded best.

Thus, the long pieces were driving the band. And to Ellington, the most important of these were his three "Sacred Concerts." Duke had gone to church regularly as a boy; indeed, frequently his parents took him to both his mother's and his father's churches on Sunday. But through the early part of his adult life he never showed much interest in religion. For one thing, traveling so much, and working so late at night, made it difficult for him to get to church with any regularity.

But then in the 1950s a certain change came over him. For one thing, his doctor decided that he was overweight and told him to go on a diet. It was not surprising that he had gotten heavy, for he had always been a big eater. He loved ice cream, and would buy four quarts at a time—he even carried a big silver spoon around with him to eat it with. Sometimes he would start a meal with ice cream, then order eggs, a steak, and finish off with more ice cream. For a period his favorite dessert was a concoction of chocolate cake, custard, ice cream, jelly, applesauce, and whipped cream. Furthermore, although Ellington did not abuse alcohol, he did like his drinks when he was relaxing. Needless to say, through much of the years after he had become successful he was overweight.

But once his doctor pointed out that carrying a lot of extra weight around put him at risk of high blood pressure and a possible heart attack, Duke decided to cut down. He went on a diet of steak, grapefruit, and black coffee, and very quickly slimmed down. He also sharply reduced his drinking; he had seen what alcohol had done to Bubber Miley and many others in the heavy drinking world of nightclubs he had spent so much time working in, and for the rest of his life he drank only moderately.

At the same time he became interested in religion again. It is hard to say that these changes in his life-style were related, but frequently shifts of this kind come along together in people's lives.

In any case, although it was still difficult for him to attend church regularly, he began to read the Bible seriously; he eventually would go through it five times, so he claimed. He started praying again, and in general began to think more about God and religion. Therefore, when he was offered the opportunity to write some religious music, he jumped at the chance.

The suggestion came in 1965 from a church in San Francisco which had just been completed, Grace Cathedral. The people in charge wanted some sort of celebration to commemorate the occasion. It occurred to them that having a jazz musician, instead of a classical composer, would be a novelty and would attract attention.

Delighted, Duke started working on the music. It would not be a single long piece, like "Black, Brown, and Beige," but a concert of individual pieces with religious themes. The main piece in this First Sacred Concert was called "In the Beginning God," and ran for about fifteen minutes. But the concert also included a version of "Come Sunday," from "Black, Brown, and Beige," some spirituals, and one called "David Danced Before the Lord with All His Might," which featured Bunny Briggs, a well-known jazz dancer.

The First Sacred Concert was a great success and was highly

publicized. Duke was encouraged to write another one, but it was 1968 before he had another chance. The Second Sacred Concert had its premier in New York at the Cathedral of St. John the Divine, one of the largest churches in the world, and again got a lot of publicity. The Third Sacred Concert was given in 1973 in an even more famous church, Westminster Abbey in London. This, too, was considered a great success.

Unfortunately, by the time of the Third Sacred Concert, Duke Ellington was very sick. The year before, when the band had been playing in Texas, Cootie Williams had come down with a chest ailment. It was decided that the whole band ought to be checked out, to be sure that nobody had caught anything from Cootie. As it turned out, there was nothing terribly wrong with most of the musicians; but two were suffering from something more serious, and were told to have further check-ups when they got home. They were Harry Carney, who had been with the band since before the Cotton Club days, and Duke Ellington.

It turned out that Duke Ellington was suffering from lung cancer. It was then, and still is, a disease that is hard to cure. Furthermore, it can take a real toll on the body, leaving the person exhausted much of the time, especially a man in his seventies, as Duke was.

But Duke Ellington had always seen himself as special, as somebody different from ordinary mortals. It did not seem to him that he ought to die, and instead of slowing down, or even winding up his career, he went on as he had always done, traveling extensively, playing and composing as usual. He did not like to think that he could no longer be master of things, and as much as possible he concealed his illness. Only his doctor and his sister, Ruth, knew about it at first, although eventually his son, Mercer, was told. Among other things, Duke was working on his Third Sacred Concert, and he was determined to hear it played in the famous Westminster Abbey. It was a struggle for him to get through it, but he managed. He returned to New York and for a few weeks tried to continue his usual course of playing and composing. Then, in January 1974 he collapsed and was rushed to a hospital. After two or three weeks he was allowed to go home to be attended there. But his condition continued to grow worse, and in April he was forced to go back into the hospital. An announcement was made that he was not suffering from anything serious, but this, of course, was not true. Nonetheless he continued to work on revising the Third Sacred Concert, with the help of Mercer. He was still in the hospital when his seventy-fifth birthday arrived. He was too sick to celebrate it, but the band was brought together to play some selections from the Second Sacred Concert. Still Duke would not give up but continued to work. It was no use, and on May 24, early in the morning, he died.

He had lived an extraordinary life. He had risen from a modest home to become one of the most renowned artists of his age. He had faced down race prejudice and had beaten it. He had traveled all over the world, mingling with princes and thieves, kings and gangsters. Always he had done things "first-class," as he put it, and along the way he had enjoyed himself immensely. He had seen the best and worst of people, the top and bottom of life. And without doubt, he had created one of the finest bodies of music made by anybody in the twentieth century.

His death was front page news worldwide. The *New York Times* gave it a front page headline: DUKE ELLINGTON, MASTER OF MUSIC, DIES AT 75. In its story it called him "America's most important composer." President Nixon issued a statement and across the country, and elsewhere in the world, there were expressions of grief. His funeral, held at the Cathedral of St.

John the Divine, where the Second Sacred Concert had first been performed, was attended by an incredible ten thousand people.

How can we sum up Duke Ellington? He was, indeed, a complex man. He was, on the one hand, egocentric, seeing himself as above others, and tending to put himself first; but he was also a very generous man, who went on supporting musicians like Sonny Greer long after they had left the band. He was devoted to his family and would do anything for them—his sister, his son, his nephews, his grandson, his father, and of course his beloved mother. But he insisted on being in charge, always the dominating force, and far too frequently he tried to tell them what they should do with their lives.

He was a genuinely religious man; but he also felt free to enjoy himself in ways that would not have been approved of by many strictly religious people. He seems to have been a mass of contradictions; but in fact the contradictions disappear when we keep in mind that he had been raised to be "special," as his mother had said, and he did not believe he was bound by the ordinary rules.

The kind of person Duke was shaped the music he made. For one thing, he had absolute faith in his own taste: If it sounded good to him, he believed it must be good. He was not always wondering if this or that melody or chord was right. If he liked it, that was enough.

For another thing, his ability to dominate the people around him made it possible for him to get the sometimes unruly people in his orchestra to do what he wanted them to do. We must remember that by the mid-1930s many of Duke's musicians were stars in the world of jazz fans and dancers who followed the bands closely. Most of them had firm ideas of how they wanted to play, and would not have taken instruction from most people. But they took it from Duke.

Duke was clever about this. He never tried to get any of his musicians to change their basic styles. Instead, he encouraged them to develop their strong points. And he was almost always right about the direction he wanted them to take. It was Duke who got Cootie to learn the plunger style which made him famous, Duke who gave Tricky Sam Nanton room to experiment with his growls, Duke who featured Jimmy Blanton on long pieces, which he had not done with any of his other bassists. He was as important in making these people stars as they were themselves.

Finally, there is what is called *charisma*. The word means a special atmosphere that seems to surround certain people, making people want to be part of their world. Duke Ellington had this quality and it was very helpful in getting people to do things the way he wanted them done. People who wanted to be part of Duke's crowd would help to see that he got good recording contracts, that he got jobs in clubs and theaters that would enhance his reputation, that he got awards, prizes, met notable people, got invited to the White House, palaces, and castles. In particular, Duke's charisma attracted musicians to him; they wanted to be in his band even when Duke was not necessarily paying the highest salaries.

Duke's music, then, grew out of his personality. And it is the music, finally, which matters—all those great records that date back to "East St. Louis Toodle-Oo" made in 1926. Because of the way Duke created his music, so often feeding it to the members of the band one at a time from the piano, he did not leave many written scores of his great pieces. In the years since his death other musicians have managed to copy these pieces onto paper from the recordings, a difficult and time-consuming task. It is therefore possible for orchestras today to sit down and play many of these famous works. But although recreations of this kind are very useful in many ways, and certainly are good training for young musicians, they never can quite capture the sound of the originals. So much of the quality of Duke's records is due to the special sounds and styles of the men in the band, that without Johnny Hodges, Cootie Williams, and the rest, the music will not quite sound the same.

The legacy Duke Ellington left us is all those great records, hundreds of them, like "Black and Tan Fantasy," "Rockin' in Rhythm," "Mood Indigo," "Creole Love Call," "Ko-Ko," "Harlem Airshaft," "Cotton Tail," and so many others.

In my own opinion, the extended pieces which became increasingly important to Duke, do not measure up to the shorter, purely jazz pieces. Critics differ on this point, and each listener must decide on his or her own. But there can be no doubt about one thing, which is that Duke Ellington, in the course of an extraordinary life, gave the world a body of music of surpassing brilliance.

FOR FURTHER STUDY

There are several books on Duke Ellington which readers interested in learning more about him and his work might find useful. One is Duke's autobiography, called *Music is My Mistress*, originally published by Doubleday, and now available in a Da Capo paperback edition. In this book Ellington is not very frank about his life and how he worked, nor is the book very well organized, but it does give Ellington's impressions of his childhood, his start in music, and other important events in his life.

Also useful is Mercer Ellington's biography of his father, called *Duke Ellington in Person* and published by Houghton Mifflin. Mercer is quite frank about his father's strengths and weaknesses, and gives a lively picture of how the band worked.

Finally, there is my own full-length study of the music master, called *Duke Ellington,* published by Oxford University Press. It is available in a paperback edition.

More important than the books are the recordings Duke left

us. As always in jazz, record stores are likely to carry only portions of any given artist's work. Fortunately, dozens of Ellington records are still in print. Most important are two long series of his early work, both issued by French companies: CBS "Aimez Vous le Jazz," *The Complete Duke Ellington;* and the RCA Black and White set called *The Works of Duke Ellington Integrale.* Together these sets comprise fifty albums and contain most of Duke's work from the late 1920s to the early 1940s. Big record stores will usually have portions of these sets.

More easily available is a three album MCA set called *The Beginning, Hot in Harlem,* and *Rockin' in Rhythm,* which contain good examples of Duke's music from the 1920s and early 1930s. Several of Duke's extended works, including the "Sacred Concerts," are usually available on records.

However, today records are being phased out in favor of CDs, and much important Ellington material is more easily available in this form. Particularly recommended are *The Eternal Ellington,* which contains examples from Duke's entire career; *The Duke 1940* vol. 1, which includes important cuts like "Ko-Ko" and "Harlem Airshaft"; and *The Great Ellington Units,* which has a good sample of the small groups. Many of the extended pieces are also out on CD, as well as the recording of the famous Newport concert.

INDEX

141